To all those in the hospitality
industry, past and present —

We've got you.

We dedicate Chefs at Home to three Hospitality Action patrons, George Goring OBE, Albert Roux OBE and Michel Roux OBE, all of whom we said goodbye to during the making of this book.

Hospitality Action

CHEFS
—— AT ——
HOME

Photography by Kris Kirkham
Illustration by David Loftus

Jon
Croft
Editions

In association with
Bloomsbury Publishing Plc

contents

Foreword

No other industry sector can boast the same
camaraderie as hospitality. We're a family, a band
of brothers and sisters. My friend Tom Kerridge calls
his team his gang of pirates, and I know exactly what
he means. We work hard together, and we play hard
together. Our sense of professional purpose is built
upon providing pleasure to others.

When lockdown began in March 2020, we all felt a
deep sense of loss, but this was tempered by the joy
of spending precious time at home with our families.

Behind our closed doors, we all did what we do
best: we cooked. And cooked. So, when Hospitality
Action asked us to contribute to *Chefs at Home*, we
had lists of recipes as long as your arm to offer up.
All the dishes in this book were conceived and
cooked with love: think butties, Monster Munch
and mash, not foams, soils and emulsions. I hope
you enjoy cooking them with your families as much
as we did with ours. And thank you: by buying this
book, you've helped Hospitality Action support our
beloved industry.

Jason Atherton
Chef-Patron & Principal Patron, Hospitality Action

Welcome to our beautiful recipe book. And thank you for supporting our wonderful charity, Hospitality Action, which exists to help hospitality people whose lives hit a bump in the road.

The world span off its axis in 2020, and hospitality was the sector worst-hit by the pandemic. At Hospitality Action, we watched on in horror as news of closures and job losses started to spread. Luckier workers were furloughed. Others tumbled into financial peril overnight.

The industry we serve faced an existential crisis.

Our phones began to ring off the hook. In the last days of March, our website saw the equivalent of three years' traffic; and, on the morning we opened our emergency grant portal, we received over 20,000 emails within the first hour.

Through the first year of the pandemic, we did all we could to raise funds to help hospitality households up and down the country, people whose livelihoods were literally disappearing.

How tough were – are – things for hospitality workers? Very. Here's David's story.

David had nine pounds and one penny in his account when we heard from him and couldn't afford to turn on his lights or his television. To make his money stretch, he was buying one potato, one tomato or one onion at a time, and rationing his gas by only cooking one meal a day. When we called him to tell him we were sending him a grant, David sang down the phone to us and danced around his kitchen.

The first lockdown of 2020 made us all realise just how much hospitality enriches our lives, and just how keenly we missed it. We play out our biggest life events in hospitality venues, from nervous first dates to joyous wedding breakfasts, and from baby showers to toasting the departed. They're where many of those moments that make life worth living take place: the morning chat with your friendly barista, the cheeky pint after work with pals, the Saturday morning soak in a warm pool, the Sunday roast with the family...

As Joni Mitchell sang, you don't know what you've got 'til it's gone.

Deprived of access to our favourite restaurants, pubs and hotels, and with time on our hands, we all rummaged in kitchen cupboards for long-forgotten tins, bags and pots and began to get creative in the kitchen – and professional chefs were no different.

On a springtime phone call, Jason Atherton and I hatched the idea of a recipe book celebrating the lockdown dishes that chefs were conjuring up at home; and we knew just the person to help us. Jon Croft is the doyen of cookery book publishing, the man who gave us the gift of Keith Floyd. I emailed him to ask if he'd like to get involved.

'Do I want to?' came Jon's response. 'It's the book I think I might have been born to publish!'

The book we've created with the assistance of Jon, his wonderful team and more than 50 outstanding chefs, isn't about haute cuisine. There are thousands of other titles on bookshop shelves you can reach for, if that's what you're after. Rather, it's about the hearty, nutritious and tasty dishes chefs were cooking for their families, while their restaurants were closed.

This is home cooking with a heart. And it's reflective of the ethnic and cultural diversity that's come to define British cuisine.

By buying this book, you're helping to put the lights back on, and food on the table, in houses like David's; and you're drawing smiles back on faces. And if that doesn't give you a healthy appetite, I don't know what will.

Happy cooking!

Mark Lewis
Chief Executive, Hospitality Action

Paul Ainsworth

Jason Atherton

Sat Bains

Tommy Banks

Nieves Barragán Moha

Michael Caines

Claire Clark

Daniel Clifford

James Cochran

Richard Corrigan

Lisa Goodwin-Allen

Elizabeth Haigh

Angela Hartnett

Anna Haugh

Mark Hix

Tom Kitchin

Atul Kochhar

Mark Lewis

Giorgio Locatelli

David Loftus

Chantelle Nicholson

Jamie Oliver

Adam O'Shepherd

Nathan Outlaw

Gordon Ramsay

Farokh Talati

Stephen Terry

Ben Tish

Cyrus Todiwala

Mitch Tonks

s Barrie

Raymond Blanc

Heston Blumenthal

Claude Bosi

Tom Brown

Croft

Thuy Diem-Pham

Calum Franklin

Chris Galvin

Robin Gill

l Howard

Niall Keating

Tom Kerridge

Selin Kiazim

Kris Kirkham

kx Majozi

James Martin

Thomasina Miers

Saiphin Moore

Naved Nasir

on Rimmer

Michel Roux Jr

Vivek Singh

Clare Smyth

Jack Stein

Usher
chard Sharples

Marcus Wareing

John Williams

Andrew Wong

Hospitality
Action

breakfast & lunch

Anna Haugh

MUSHROOMS ON TOAST
with boiled eggs

For me this is the only way to serve mushrooms on toast. The perfect kick-start to your morning even before you've had your first sip of coffee. Packed full of protein, this delicious, fuss-free dish also boasts one of your five a day. With little washing up, you'll return to it again and again for breakfast, brunch or lunch.

Serves 4

350g mixed mushrooms, sliced
2 tablespoons olive oil
1 teaspoon salt
pinch of freshly ground pepper or chilli flakes,
    plus extra to serve if needed
4 eggs

To finish
4 slices of sourdough, toasted
4 teaspoons salted butter
bunch of tarragon, leaves picked

Preheat the oven to 180°C/160°C fan/Gas mark 4 and bring a saucepan of water to the boil.

Place the mushrooms in a bowl and add the olive oil, salt and pepper (or chilli flakes), and mix to coat. Spread the mushrooms on a baking tray and bake for 10 minutes, until cooked and they have taken on some colour.

Meanwhile, carefully lower the eggs into the saucepan and boil for 6 minutes. When cooked, remove from the water with a slotted spoon, then tap the shells gently to break them open. Dip the eggs in a bowl of cold water so they are not too hot to peel, then peel and cut in half. Set aside.

Butter the toast, divide the mushrooms on top and scatter with equal amounts of the tarragon leaves. Place the halved eggs on top, dividing them equally between the slices of toast, then add a little extra black pepper or chilli flakes if you want.

Farokh Talati

PARSI OMELETTE

The Parsis have a love affair with the egg! This is a typical café-style omelette, which is incredibly easy to make at home, and based on my favourite breakfast in Mumbai at Café Colony in the Parsi colony at Dadar. A well-seasoned cast-iron or non-stick pan is essential to ensure that your omelette comes away from the pan in one piece.

The ginger-garlic paste makes more than you need for this recipe, but it will keep in the fridge to use in curries. Alternatively, freeze it in ice-cube trays and then just pop it in the pan frozen – it will take seconds to defrost.

Serves 1

2 tablespoons ghee or vegetable oil
1 shallot or ½ small red onion, finely diced
1 small green chilli, thinly sliced
1 teaspoon dhansak masala
½ teaspoon garam masala
¼ teaspoon ground turmeric
3 large eggs, beaten with a pinch of salt
2 tablespoons grated cheese (whatever you may have lurking in the back of your fridge)
2 tablespoons chopped coriander, plus extra to serve
salt

For the ginger-garlic paste
100g fresh ginger root, peeled
5 large garlic cloves, peeled
2 tablespoons vegetable oil
1 teaspoon salt

To serve
lemon wedge
warm toast or rotli
a few slices of red onion

First, make the ginger-garlic paste. Blitz all the ingredients together in a food processor to a coarse consistency. Set aside until needed, or freeze.

Heat the ghee or oil in a frying pan over a medium heat and add the shallots or onion, chilli and 2 teaspoons of the ginger-garlic paste. Sizzle for a few minutes with a pinch of salt until the shallots or onion begin to brown, then add both the masalas and turmeric and stir together for another 30 seconds.

Pour in the eggs and quickly mix all ingredients together in the pan. Gently agitate or stir the egg mixture from the bottom of the pan, allowing the runny egg from the top to seep to the bottom and gently set before agitating again. Continue this process for the next minute, until you have a semi-set custard-like wobble on the top of the pan, then sprinkle the cheese and the coriander over the top.

Now it's time to flip your omelette: you must let the omelette know you are in control and mean business. Firmly hold the handle and give the pan some assertive nudges, jiggles and taps to loosen the omelette from the base. Then, using a spatula, fold the omelette over on itself, encasing the cheese and coriander (I bring 3 o'clock over to 9 o'clock so that the pan handle is not in the way when turning out the omelette. Bring the pan to plate and turn out the omelette in a quick and confident motion.

Squeeze a healthy wedge of lemon over the top and serve with hot buttered rotli or toast, a sprinkle more of coriander and slices of raw red onion.

Tommy Banks

CHORIZO & MOZZARELLA SHAKSHUKA

I love shakshuka – it's so easy, and so, so tasty. I made this a lot in lockdown for a brunch. I live on a farm, so I'd always be up early in the morning seeing what was ready to be harvested that day, or enjoying the quiet moments with my dog, Socks. The result was that I often skipped breakfast and had something a little later on in the morning. This recipe is super-quick, and I love loading it up on to hot, buttered, sourdough toast.

Serves 4

drizzle of olive oil
1 red onion, diced
1 garlic clove, crushed
about 250g chorizo, cut into 5mm slices
1 teaspoon ground cumin
1 teaspoon paprika
2 red peppers, deseeded and sliced
1 mild red chilli, sliced (deseeded if you
     want less heat)
1 x 400g tin of chopped tomatoes
1 tablespoon Worcestershire sauce
4 eggs
1 x 125g ball of mozzarella, sliced
1 bunch of coriander, finely chopped
salt and freshly ground black pepper
toasted sourdough bread, to serve

Drizzle the oil into a lidded casserole dish on a medium–high heat. Add the onion and garlic and allow to sweat for about 5 minutes, until soft. Add in the chorizo, cumin and paprika, and cook for another 1 minute.

Add the peppers and chilli and allow to cook for another couple of minutes, until they're slightly softened. Then, add the chopped tomatoes and Worcestershire sauce. Give everything a good stir and season well. Allow the sauce to bubble for about 8–10 minutes, until it thickens slightly.

Turn down the heat and use the back of a spoon to make 4 wells in the sauce. Crack 1 egg into each well and place mozzarella slices in the gaps in between. Put the lid on the casserole dish, and allow the eggs to cook gently for about 7–10 minutes – you want your whites to be set, but the yolk runny.

Remove the lid, scatter over the chopped coriander and serve with buttered toasted sourdough.

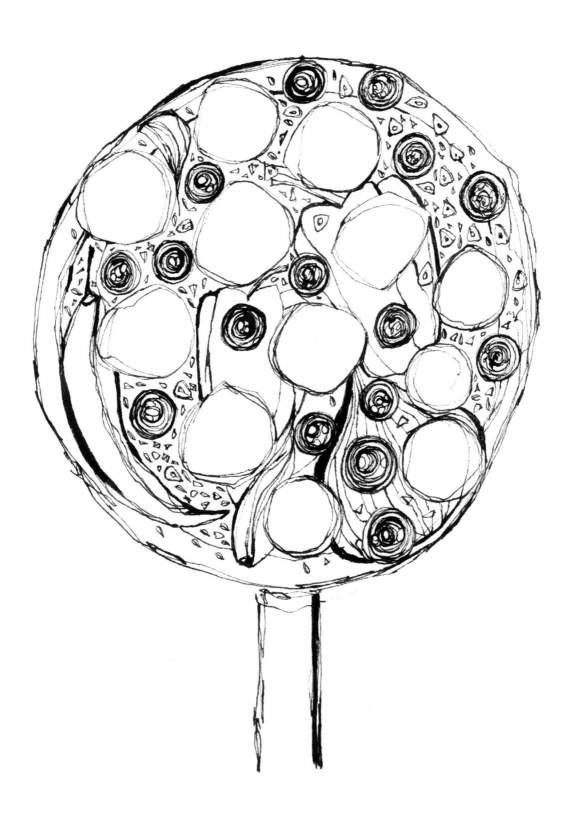

BARRIE BAKED BEANS
with treacle bread

During lockdown, I was putting together breakfast boxes for my outdoor reared pork farm in Anglesey, The Fat Pig Farm. And you can't send out top bacon, sausage and black pudding without proper beans, so I created this recipe. It was a massive hit and when we opened our pop up in the summer we decided to offer breakfast too; the beans were the talking point ... and the pork of course!

Serves 2–3

For the treacle bread
130g starter (see Chef's notes, page 19)
200g strong white bread flour, plus extra
    for dusting
85ml water
30g treacle
1 teaspoon salt
50/50 mixture of rice flour and cornflour,
    for dusting
polenta, for dusting
olive oil, for drizzling

For the beans
200g dried cannellini beans, soaked
    overnight in cold water
½ onion, peeled
½ carrot, peeled
4 garlic cloves, crushed
5 black peppercorns
5 thyme sprigs
2 rosemary sprigs
2 teaspoons salt

For the sauce
50g unsalted butter, plus an extra 30g
    to finish
1 shallot, diced
4 garlic cloves, crushed
½ red chilli, deseeded and diced
1 red pepper, deseeded and diced
1 teaspoon smoked paprika
1 teaspoon ground coriander

Two days before you intend to eat your treacle bread, feed your starter and mix it well, then leave it overnight. The following day, put the starter, flour and water in a stand mixer fitted with the dough hook. Knead it on low speed for 5 minutes, then allow it to rest for 20 minutes. Add the treacle and salt and knead for a further 10 minutes on the lowest speed, until it comes together in a dough. Remove the dough from the mixer and wrap it in a clean tea towel. Leave it to rest for 20 minutes, then take it out and fold it over on itself, then wrap it and leave it again. Do this about 9 or 10 times altogether. Then, place the dough in a bowl, cover it and leave it in the fridge for at least 3 hours. The rise won't be huge in this time, so don't worry if it seems barely noticeable – it's all about getting the structure in the bread.

Shape the dough into a loaf, working the tension in the dough, stretching and folding as you're shaping it, then finally flip it over and tuck in the corners. Dust a round, cane bread basket (large enough to hold an 800g–1kg loaf), or suitable bowl, with the rice flour/cornflour mixture and strong bread flour, and place the dough into the dusted basket. Dust with polenta. Leave the shaped dough to prove in the fridge overnight – this time the bread should rise enough to more or less fill the basket.

Make the beans. Drain the soaked beans and add them to a saucepan with the onion, carrot, garlic, peppercorns, thyme, rosemary and 1 litre of water. Place the pan over a high heat and bring the water to the boil. Skim away any impurities as they rise to the surface and, after 10 minutes' boiling, add the salt (if you add the salt or any acidity at the start, you can toughen the skins of the beans). Lower the heat so you have a rolling simmer and cook the beans for about 1½ hours, until tender. Then, drain them in a sieve and allow to cool. Discard everything except for the beans and set aside.

Make the sauce. Melt the butter in a saucepan over a medium–low heat. Add the shallot, garlic, chilli and pepper, season with a pinch of salt, and sweat for about 8–10 minutes, until soft. Add the paprika and coriander and stir until fragrant. Add the tomato purée, cook for 5 minutes, then add the chicken stock, honey, sugar and vinegar and bring to a simmer. Add the bay leaf, simmer

3 tablespoons tomato purée
100ml chicken stock
2 tablespoons local honey
50g caster sugar
50ml white wine vinegar
1 bay leaf
½ bunch of flat-leaf parsley, leaves
    and stalks chopped
salt and freshly ground black pepper

for about 10 minutes, then add the cooked cannellini beans. Simmer for a further 10 minutes, then season with salt and pepper to taste. Keep warm until needed.

Preheat the oven to 260°C/240°C fan/Gas mark 9 with a baking tray half-filled with water in the base (this will create a burst of steam when you first put the bread in the oven to help it form a delicious crust).

Turn out the dough on to a baking tray and score the top, making two deep slashes in it with a bread scorer or sharp knife, or make two big cuts with scissors. Bake the loaf for 15 minutes, until it has developed a dark crust and the base sounds hollow when tapped. Remove it from the oven and place on a wire rack to cool.

Remove the bay leaf from the beans and discard. Add the parsley and butter and stir through.

Heat a griddle pan to hot. Slice the bread and drizzle the slices with olive oil. Place the slices on the hot griddle pan until charred (you want to get those scorched bar marks), then remove to plates and serve with the beans piled on top.

Chef's notes: the sourdough starter

First, get yourself a small glass jar and make sure it is totally clean. Weigh it and make a note of the weight (without the lid). Then, in the jar...
  Day 1: Mix 175ml water with 75g full-fat yoghurt. Cover the top of the jar tightly with cling film. Set aside at room temperature. **Day 2:** Add 120g strong white bread flour and mix to combine. Cover again with cling film and set aside. **Day 3:** A day of rest – leave your starter at cool room temperature for a whole day. **Day 4:** Add 300ml water and 30g more full-fat yoghurt. Mix to combine, cover and set aside. **Day 5:** Add 150g strong white bread flour and 150ml water and mix well. Cover again and set aside. At this point you should notice a higher rise in your jar and more aeration in the mixture. This lets you know that your starter is alive and kicking. **Day 6:** Weigh the mixture: place the whole jar on the scales and deduct the weight of the jar. Now you know how much your starter weighs. Remove half of it from the jar and discard. Then, add back the same weight in strong white bread flour and the same weight in water. For example, if your leftover starter weighs 175g, add 175g flour and 175ml water. Your starter is now ready to use. Weigh out the amount you need for your recipe, then work out the remaining weight in the jar and feed it again, with equal amounts of the flour and of the water, to keep it going.

Angela Hartnett

BACON & FRIED EGG BUN

During the lockdown Neil, my husband, and I cooked many meals for the NHS. Neil would always make these breakfast buns for the troops, and, in my opinion, there's nothing better than enjoying them with lots of brown sauce – it's the way forward!

Serves 6

12 bacon rashers
good knob of unsalted butter
6 free-range eggs (I use Burford Browns or Fluffetts)
6 plain white rolls or baps, sliced in half and buttered
salt and freshly ground black pepper
sauce of choice (such as brown sauce or tomato ketchup), to serve

Preheat the oven to 200°C/180°C fan/Gas mark 6.

Lay the bacon rashers in a single layer on a baking tray and cook them for 8 minutes, turning halfway through the cooking time, until nice and crispy.

At the same time add the butter to a large frying pan (or use 2 pans if you don't have one big enough to hold all the eggs). Allow the butter to bubble gently, then crack the eggs into the pan and fry for 2–3 minutes, until the whites start to crisp at the edge but the yolks are still soft. Use a spoon to coat the top of the egg with the hot butter while it's cooking, and season with salt and pepper.

When the eggs are ready, place the bacon in the buttered baps and add the seasoned egg. Finish with your choice of sauce and dig in.

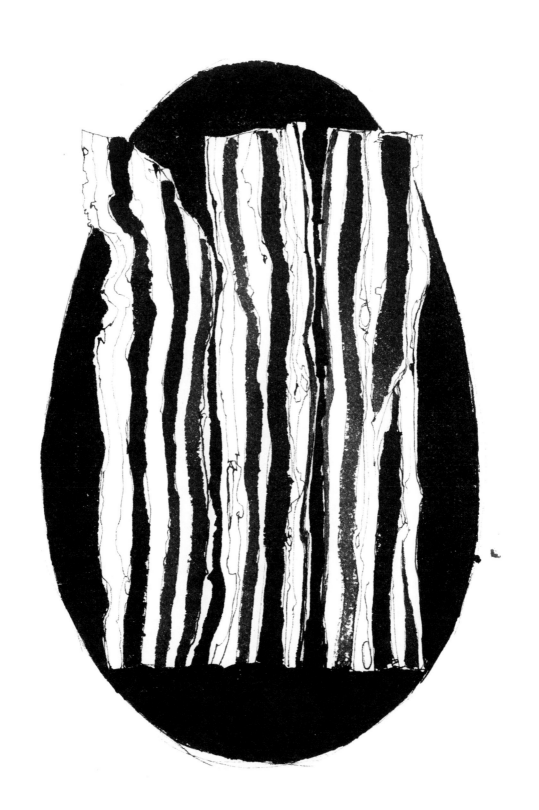

KEDGEREE

This is such a brilliant kedgeree – and not just for breakfast or brunch, but at any time. It's a little different to the more traditional versions, but it's well worth the effort. And, although it has several components, you can prepare them ahead so all you have to do is finish off the dish just before serving. I've used pearl barley instead of rice and there's a lovely, spicy sauce to mix through. I love to add a poached egg and diced apple over the top to maximise the flavours and textures.

Serves 4

400ml whole milk
4 black peppercorns
2 bay leaves
2 garlic cloves, crushed
1 thyme sprig, leaves picked
250g smoked mackerel fillets
olive oil
1 shallot, finely chopped
1 teaspoon Madras curry powder
½ teaspoon ground turmeric
200g pearl barley, well rinsed
100ml dry white wine
250ml good-quality chicken stock
    (ideally homemade)
white wine vinegar, for poaching
4 eggs, at room temperature
sea salt and freshly cracked black pepper

For the curry sauce
30g unsalted butter
sunflower or vegetable oil
250g onions, chopped
1 tablespoon brown mustard seeds
1 red pepper, deseeded and sliced
1 teaspoon Madras curry powder
200ml good-quality chicken stock
    (ideally homemade)
200ml full-fat coconut milk
1 banana, chopped
2 teaspoons chopped coriander stalks
juice of ½ lime

First make the curry sauce. Heat a heavy-based saucepan with a tight-fitting lid over a medium–high heat. Add the butter and a splash of oil and allow the butter to melt. When the butter is foaming, add the onions and sauté for 3 minutes, then add the mustard seeds, red pepper and curry powder and continue sautéing until the vegetables are tender.

Stir in the chicken stock and leave it to bubble until it evaporates. Add the coconut milk and bring to the boil, then add the banana and coriander stalks. Turn off the heat and leave the mixture to infuse, covered, for at least 1 hour but up to 1 day if you keep it in the fridge in a sealed container.

Once the sauce has infused, transfer it to a blender or food processor and blitz until smooth. Pass the sauce through a fine sieve, season lightly with salt and pepper and the lime juice, and set aside. When the sauce is completely cool, cover and chill until needed.

Meanwhile, poach the mackerel. Place the milk in another heavy-based saucepan and bring to a simmer. Add the peppercorns, bay leaves, garlic and thyme, and leave to simmer for 10 minutes. Add the mackerel and continue simmering for 5 minutes, or until the flesh flakes easily. Remove the pan from the heat and leave the fillets to cool completely in the milk.

When the mackerel is cool, strain the milk into a bowl and measure out and set aside 250ml of it. Rinse the mackerel and pat it dry, then remove and discard the skin and any bones. Flake the flesh into large pieces and set aside in a bowl until required. If not using immediately, add a small amount of the poaching liquid to keep it moist.

Start cooking the barley about 1 hour before you plan to serve. Heat another heavy-based pan over a medium–high heat, then add a splash of oil. When hot, add the shallot and stir for 2 minutes. Stir in the curry powder and turmeric and continue stirring until the shallots are tender (about 2 minutes). Stir in the barley, then add the wine, stirring to deglaze the pan, and leave it to boil until it evaporates. Add the chicken stock,

To finish
1 green apple
40g parmesan, freshly grated
10g unsalted butter
1 teaspoon freshly squeezed lemon juice
chopped coriander leaves

reduce the heat a little and simmer for 45 minutes, stirring frequently, or until the barley is tender. At this point, you can set the dish aside to finish cooking just before serving.

Meanwhile, poach the eggs. Bring a large pan of water to the boil. Add a splash of vinegar and turn down the heat so the water is barely simmering. One by one, carefully crack each egg into a cup and then lower and release it into the water. Poach for 3–4 minutes, until the whites are set. Use a slotted spoon to remove each egg from the water and set aside while you make the remainder.

When you're ready to finish cooking, stir the curry sauce into the barley and reheat, if necessary.

Halve, core and finely chop the apple.

Just before you're ready to serve, gently stir one-third of the smoked mackerel, the parmesan, butter and lemon juice into the barley. Garnish with the remaining smoked mackerel, and the chopped apple and coriander. Divide the kedgeree between 4 serving plates, top each with a poached egg and sprinkle with cracked pepper.

POWER OMELETTE

Power up your mornings with my take on the classic omelette. The pairing of bacon, spicy chorizo, red pepper and red onion submerged in six whole eggs, coupled with a chilli avocado side and a helping of cottage cheese, will put meat on your bones and help you to tackle whatever the day brings.

Serves 2

olive oil
2 rashers of back bacon, chopped into lardons
100g chorizo, chopped
1 long red pepper, deseeded and sliced
1 red onion, sliced
6 eggs, lightly beaten
1 avocado
chilli flakes, to taste
salt and freshly ground black pepper
100g cottage cheese, to serve

Drizzle a little olive oil into a large non-stick frying pan and set over a medium heat. When hot, add the bacon and chorizo and sweat for a few minutes, until caramelised. Add the pepper and onion and cook for about 3–5 minutes, until soft.

Season the beaten eggs with salt and pepper, then add them to the pan. Cook gently, moving the outside of the eggs to the centre to incorporate all the ingredients, on a low heat for about 15 minutes, until the omelette is mostly set with a slight wobble in the middle.

Meanwhile, halve and destone the avocado and scoop the flesh into a bowl. Sprinkle with salt, pepper and chilli flakes, to taste, and drizzle with a little olive oil.

Once the omelette is ready, turn off the heat and allow it to rest and set fully for a few minutes. Cut the omelette like a tart and serve it with the avocado mixture and a dollop of cottage cheese.

Atul Kochhar

JAMSHEDPUR-STYLE EGG ROLLS

I was born and raised in Jamshedpur, in the east Indian state of Jharkhand, and I've woven these early influences into this recipe. The scent of coriander, chilli powder, garlic and turmeric frying remind me of being a child, and these egg rolls are a homage to this time gone by.

Serves 4

For the dough
250g plain flour
4–5 tablespoons sunflower oil
4 eggs, beaten
salt

For the filling
1 tablespoon sunflower oil
4 garlic cloves, sliced
4–5 large portobello mushrooms, sliced
1 tablespoon ground coriander
1 teaspoon chilli powder
¼ teaspoon ground turmeric
½ bunch of coriander, leaves picked
    and chopped
1 red onion, finely sliced
1 small cucumber, halved lengthways,
    deseeded and finely sliced
1 celery stick, finely sliced (optional)
2 tablespoons lemon juice
salt

To serve
mixed salad leaves
a few coriander leaves
8 teaspoons spicy tomato ketchup or chutney

Make the dough. Mix the flour, 2 tablespoons of the oil and a little salt together with 120ml of water to make a soft dough. Leave it to rest for 10–15 minutes, then divide it into 4 equal pieces. Shape each piece into a ball. On a lightly floured surface, roll out each ball into a disc about 2–3mm thick. Heat a frying pan over a high heat. When hot, one at a time, add the dough discs and fry until cooked through and golden brown. Set each aside on a plate while you cook the next.

Once you've cooked all the breads, add some of the remaining oil to the frying pan. One by one, dip the cooked breads in the beaten egg and pan fry for 20–30 seconds on each side, until the egg is cooked. Wrap the breads in a clean kitchen cloth to keep warm while you make the filling.

Heat the oil in a pan over a low heat and add the garlic. Sauté for a couple of minutes, until softened (taking care it doesn't burn), then add the mushrooms. Add the coriander, chilli, turmeric and a little salt, and toss everything on a high heat until the spices are well distributed, but the mushrooms still retain their texture. Add the coriander leaves and set aside.

Mix together the onion, cucumber and celery and toss them with lemon juice. Season with salt to taste.

Place the egg-coated breads on a chopping board. One by one, place equal amounts of the mushroom mixture on top, then the onion mixture. To serve, top with a few salad leaves and sprinkle with coriander leaves. Drizzle over 2 teaspoons of ketchup or chutney, then fold the bread into a roll. Cut in half and serve with more tomato ketchup or chutney alongside.

Lisa Goodwin-Allen

GOOD OLD SAUSAGE ROLL

My son Teddy-Ray and I enjoyed making these together during lockdown – he loves them!

Makes 4

240g pork sausagemeat
50g smoked pancetta, finely diced
80g mature cheddar, cut into 1cm cubes
   (I used Black Cow)
1 teaspoon wholegrain mustard
plain flour, for dusting
250g good-quality puff pastry
2 egg yolks, beaten

Place the sausagemeat, smoked pancetta, cheese and mustard in a mixing bowl and mix together until combined. Transfer to a large disposable piping bag.

On a lightly floured surface, roll out the puff pastry to a 30 x 14cm rectangle about 5mm thick.

Turn the pastry so that a long side is closest to you. Brush along the closest edge with the beaten egg. Cut 3cm off the bottom of the piping bag and pipe the sausagemeat in the centre of the pastry, from left to right, along the length. Take hold of the top edge of the pastry and fold it downwards over the filling, bringing the edges together to meet. Press down with your hand to seal the pastry edges together, then use the back of a floured fork to lightly crimp the edge. Cut along the crimped edge to neaten, leaving a 1.5cm lip.

Brush the sausage roll all over with the remaining beaten egg and carefully transfer the roll to a greased non-stick baking tray. Refrigerate for at least 30 minutes to firm up before cooking.

While the sausage roll is chilling, preheat the oven to 210°C/190°C fan/Gas mark 6–7.

Bake the sausage roll for 15–20 minutes, until the sausagemeat is cooked through, and the pastry is puffed up and golden (it should read 73°C on a meat thermometer). Remove from the oven and transfer to a wire rack to rest for 10 minutes. Cut on an angle into 4 even-sized pieces and serve warm.

Cyrus Todiwala

1833 CHEESE BITES

Why 1833? Because I used the famous Barber's 1833 special cheddar. You can, of course, use another good-quality cheddar if you can't get 1833, but please do not use any processed cheese. These biscuits are great any time of the day and not just moreish, but addictive.

Makes about 30 biscuits

200g plain flour, plus extra for dusting
120g unsalted butter, cubed and chilled
1 teaspoon caraway seeds, partly crushed
good pinch of salt
100g 1833 cheddar, grated
ice-cold water
1 egg, beaten (optional)

Sift the flour into a bowl, then add the cubed butter, caraway seeds and salt. Combine the mixture, rubbing the butter into the flour, until the butter softens slightly but not so that it becomes too soft – you're looking for a breadcrumb consistency. Then, stir in the cheese. Gradually add a little ice-cold water until you get a good, firm dough.

Work the dough gently until it all comes together, then form it into a ball and place it in a bowl with a lid. Refrigerate for at least 30 minutes.

Preheat the oven to 140°C/120°C fan/Gas mark 1.

Turn out the dough on to a lightly floured surface and roll it out until 5mm thick. Cut the dough into pieces roughly 4–5cm in diameter. Re-roll the trimmings (handle them gently, though) to repeat the process until you have used up all the dough and have about 30 biscuits. You may wish to brush the tops with the beaten egg before baking, but it's not necessary.

Transfer the biscuits to a baking sheet lined with baking paper and bake until light golden (about 10 minutes), then turn off the oven and leave the biscuits inside to dry out and get a deeper colour.

Remove from the oven, leave to cool, then transfer to an airtight container to store. Enjoy as necessary – although they are dangerously moreish, so you may need to restrict yourself!

Thuy Diem Pham

LEMONGRASS CHICKEN BÁNH MÌ

Bánh mì is the most famous of Vietnam's street food dishes, and this recipe is for one of my absolute favourite fillings. It's famous for a reason: once you've had a bite of a bánh mì, no other sandwich will ever be the same again – that's a promise!

Serves 2–4 (depending on hunger)

400g chicken breast fillets, sliced diagonally into 1cm strips
2 small baguettes, or 1 large baguette cut in 2
4 teaspoons unsalted butter
6 teaspoons mayonnaise
8 teaspoons chicken liver pâté
30ml vegetable oil
1 cucumber, deseeded and cut into thick slices
4 coriander sprigs
2 spring onions, sliced lengthways
4 teaspoons light soy sauce
½ red chilli, deseeded and sliced
2 teaspoons crispy fried shallots
large pinch of crushed black peppercorns

For the carrot and daikon pickle
125ml rice vinegar
125g granulated sugar
2 medium carrots, peeled and cut into fine matchsticks
⅓ medium daikon (around 125g), peeled and cut into fine matchsticks

For the marinade
1 teaspoon light soy sauce
½ teaspoon fish sauce
½ teaspoon oyster sauce
½ tablespoon granulated sugar
½ teaspoon runny honey
2 lemongrass stalks, finely chopped
5 garlic cloves, finely chopped
2 chillies, finely chopped
3 spring onions, white part only, finely chopped
2 tablespoons sesame oil

First, make the carrot and daikon pickle. Heat the rice vinegar and sugar in a saucepan over a medium heat, stirring until the sugar has dissolved. Remove from the heat and leave to cool completely. Put the carrots and daikon in a jar, then pour over the cooled vinegar mixture. Seal the jar with a lid and place in the fridge for at least 1 day or up to 5 days to pickle before using. (The recipe will make more than you need, but you can store it for up to 2 weeks in a sterilised container in the fridge.)

Make the marinade. Combine all the marinade ingredients in a large bowl. Add the sliced chicken, mixing together well. Cover and leave in the fridge to marinate for at least 3 hours, or ideally overnight.

Preheat the oven to 180°C/160°C fan/Gas mark 4 and warm the baguettes for 2–3 minutes. Remove from the oven and cut down the centre. Pull out enough of the insides of the baguettes to make room for the fillings. Spread the butter on one side of each baguette, then top with mayonnaise. Spread the pâté on the other side.

Heat the oil in a frying pan over a medium heat until it reaches 160°C. An easy way to tell when the oil is ready is to place the tip of a wooden chopstick into it; when bubbles form on the surface of the oil, it is ready. Add the chicken strips and all of the marinade to the pan, and stir-fry for 10–12 minutes, or until the chicken is golden and cooked through. Keep the chicken moving at all times as the sugar in the marinade can burn easily. Take the chicken out of the pan and leave to one side to cool slightly.

Now it's time to layer up. Add the cucumber, pickled carrot and daikon, a generous amount of chicken, coriander and spring onion to the baguette. Drizzle over the soy sauce and sprinkle with chilli, crispy fried shallots and crushed black peppercorns, then serve. (You can halve the baguettes to serve 4, if you're not as hungry.)

Niall Keating

FRENCH DIP SANDWICHES

If the photo doesn't inspire you to make these sandwiches, I don't know what will! Far from dainty, these luscious steak and cheese sarnies drenched in a delicious gravy will keep hunger at bay as you try your best not to scoff the lot!

Serves 4

400g rib-eye steak
olive oil
4 hoagie rolls, or any suitable bread roll,
    sliced in half
6 slices of Swiss cheese
salt and freshly ground black pepper

For the gravy
¼ onion, sliced
1 garlic clove
1 small thyme sprig
1 teaspoon Worcestershire sauce
500ml beef stock

Preheat the oven to 200°C/180°C fan/Gas mark 6.

Rub the beef with olive oil, season with salt and pepper and place it in an oven- and hob-proof pan. Roast it in the oven for 20 minutes, or until the beef registers 60°C on a meat thermometer. Rest the beef, removing to a side plate, and in the meantime reducing the oven temperature to 180°C/160°C fan/Gas mark 4.

Make the gravy. Place the roasting pan with all the meat juices on the hob over a medium heat. Add the onion, garlic and whole thyme sprig and cook gently for 8–10 minutes, until the onion is soft and the mixture is fragrant.

Deglaze the pan with the Worcestershire sauce and beef stock and bring the liquid up to a simmer. Allow the sauce to bubble away until it reduces to your desired consistency – ideally, so that it coats the back of a spoon.

Thinly slice the beef and divide the slices between the hoagie rolls. Top with the slices of Swiss cheese, place the buns in a roasting tray (bun lids too – cut sides upward) and bake them in the oven until the cheese is nicely melty – about 3–4 minutes. Remove from the oven and top with the bun lids.

Pass the jus through a chinois or fine sieve and serve on the side as a dip for your sandwiches.

CRAB CRUMPET
with cauliflower & parmesan

I love this dish – for me it combines the nostalgia of cauliflower cheese and a good crumpet with a dash of added decadence. My brilliant chef James Toth came up with the recipe and it's been a favourite ever since. You'll need 10cm-diameter crumpet rings (they are easily available online) or you can use deep, 10cm biscuit/pastry cutters.

If you have any extra cauliflower purée left over, it can be frozen and is delicious served with roasted meat or fish.

Serves 6 as a starter

For the crumpets
500g plain flour
10g active dried yeast
1 tablespoon sea salt
1 teaspoon bicarbonate of soda
1 teaspoon caster sugar
600ml lukewarm water
vegetable oil, for greasing
240g fresh white crab meat
chopped chives, to serve

For the cauliflower cheese purée
250g unsalted butter, diced, plus extra
    for toasting
2 shallots, roughly chopped
4 garlic cloves, crushed
1 cauliflower, roughly chopped
75ml whole milk
75ml double cream
6 thyme sprigs
2 tablespoons Dijon mustard
4 tablespoons Worcestershire sauce
80g parmesan, grated, plus extra to serve
salt

To make the crumpets, whisk the flour, yeast, salt, bicarbonate of soda, sugar and water together in a bowl until you have a smooth batter. Put the mixture in a warm place and allow it to prove until it has doubled in size and bubbles have formed – the more bubbles the better!

Grease the insides of six 10cm crumpet rings or round cutters with a little bit of oil, then place the rings in a non-stick pan set over a medium heat and leave the rings to get hot. Heat the grill to high.

Ladle the crumpet mixture into the rings, leaving a 1cm gap between the surface of the mixture and the top of the ring to stop overflow. Leave for about 3 minutes, until the crumpets are cooked on the outside. Then, carefully remove the rings and place the crumpets on an oven tray and finish cooking them under the grill for about 3–4 minutes, until golden brown. Set aside.

Make the cauliflower cheese purée. Melt the butter in a large pan over a medium heat. Once the butter has started to foam and turn brown, add the shallots and garlic and cook for 8–10 minutes, until caramelised. Add the cauliflower and allow the cauliflower to caramelise too (about 10–15 minutes). Don't be afraid to scrape any of the sediment from the bottom of the pan into the mixture – this is all just extra flavour.

Add the milk, cream and thyme, then bring the liquid to a simmer, and simmer for about 10 minutes, until the cauliflower is cooked through. Drain the cauliflower in a sieve, collecting the liquid in a bowl underneath. Then, press the cauliflower through the sieve into a clean bowl.

Mix the remaining purée ingredients into the bowl with the cauliflower until completely combined. Using a hand-held stick blender, blend the mixture for a good 6–8 minutes until super smooth. At this point, if the purée seems too thick, add some of the reserved cooking liquid to loosen it up. Taste and season with salt if necessary.

Heat the grill again and warm up the crumpets, topped with a knob of butter, until they are nicely toasted.

Mix together the white crab meat and warm cauliflower purée, but don't add too much purée – you want just enough to bind the two together. Season if necessary and finish with finely chopped chives.

Pile the crab mixture equally on top of each crumpet and place it under the grill one more time to warm through. Once warmed, sprinkle over some parmesan, and serve.

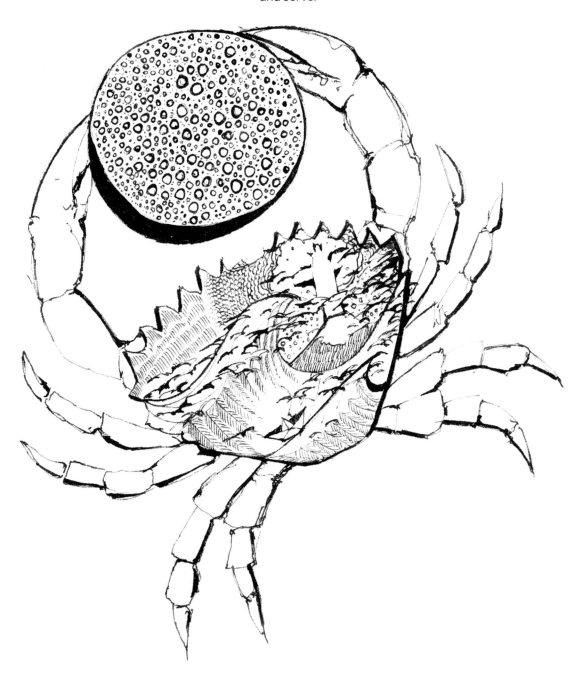

THE CROQUE MADAME

The Croque Madame is a proper Sunday brunch-style treat, and one of my favourite things to eat. In difficult times, food can be a comfort and a joy. For me rarebit is the perfect weekend treat, packing amazing flavours – you get the tanginess of the rarebit (I recommend using a good-quality strong cheddar), lovely crusty bread, cooked ham and an oozy egg. It's the ultimate comfort food.

I tend to be pretty generous with the rarebit sauce here, but if you have any leftover you can freeze it for another day. Just defrost overnight and it's ready to use the next day. Any leftover Marmite butter is great to top steaks or used in pasta dishes.

Serves 4

8 large slices of good-quality sourdough bread
200g salted butter
8 slices of good-quality ham
vegetable oil
4 rich-yolk eggs
4 pickled baby gherkins, halved widthways

For the Cornish rarebit
675g 1-year-old Davidstow or other
   mature cheddar
150ml whole milk
25g plain flour
55g fresh white breadcrumbs
1 tablespoon English mustard powder
2 whole eggs
2 egg yolks
1 tablespoon Worcestershire sauce
salt and white pepper

For the sundried tomato and Marmite butter
1 x 150g jar of sundried tomatoes, drained
   and chopped
1 tablespoon Marmite
250g salted butter, softened at room
   temperature
good squeeze of lemon juice, to taste

Make the rarebit. Slowly melt the cheese and milk together in a heavy-based saucepan, stirring continuously over a medium heat. Season with salt and white pepper. Add the flour, breadcrumbs and mustard powder, and stir continuously for about 1–2 minutes, until you get a thick consistency. Pour out the mixture on to a large baking tray and allow to cool to room temperature. Once cool, transfer the mixture to a food processor and blitz until smooth. Add the whole eggs and egg yolks through the feed tube, then, once everything is combined, add the Worcestershire sauce. Place the rarebit into a piping bag and leave at room temperature until needed.

Prepare the sundried tomato and Marmite butter. Mix the sundried tomatoes and Marmite into the softened butter until fully incorporated, then add the lemon juice to taste. Set aside at room temperature until you're ready to assemble.

Preheat the oven to 180°C/160°C fan/Gas mark 4. To build your croques, brush both sides of each slice of sourdough with the Marmite butter.

Heat a frying pan over a medium–high heat. Add 50g of the butter and leave to melt until foaming. Add 2 slices of the sourdough and fry until slightly light brown on the underside. Turn over and repeat on the other side, then set aside. Repeat with the remaining slices of sourdough, two at a time, using 50g of butter each time.

Pipe rarebit on to 1 slice of the browned sourdough, then place a couple of ham slices on top and top with another slice of sourdough. Repeat for the remaining rarebit, ham and slices of sourdough. Transfer the sandwiches to a baking tray and bake them until the cheese has melted and the sourdough is nicely toasted.

While the croque madames are cooking, heat a little vegetable oil in a frying pan over a low–medium heat. Crack in the eggs and fry until the whites are cooked and you have a nice, runny yolk.

Remove the cooked croques from the oven and place one on each serving plate. Top with a fried egg, and garnish with gherkins. Enjoy!

FISH FINGER SANDWICH
with curried mushy peas

This recipe was a bit of fun during lockdown, cooking with my son Acey. We had a little fish leftover from a Flying Fish At Home box and I wanted to make Acey a treat that he could help cook. The kid-friendly crumb coating is instead of traditional breadcrumbs – get everyone involved in the crumbling. Feel free to reduce the spicing, as not everyone likes it as spicy as we do. I've chosen to do one fat fish finger, which is easier to cook, but it would work as slimmer fish fingers too.

Serves 2

8 water biscuits
12 pickled onion Monster Munch (about 1 regular packet)
4 tablespoons rolled oats
1 teaspoon curry powder
1 teaspoon garam masala
½ teaspoon garlic powder
2–3 tablespoons plain flour
2 eggs, beaten
2 x 100g skinless, boneless haddock or cod fillets
60ml vegetable oil
50g unsalted butter
juice of ⅓ lemon

For the mushy peas
50g unsalted butter
150g frozen peas
2cm piece of fresh ginger, peeled and finely diced
1 green chilli, sliced (deseeded if you want)
1 teaspoon garlic powder
1 teaspoon garam masala
1 teaspoon curry powder
1 avocado
1 tablespoon chopped mint leaves

To serve
2 breakfast muffins, sliced in half
few dashes of hot sauce, to taste
1 tablespoon mayonnaise

First, crunch the water biscuits and Monster Munch together with your hands in a bowl until you have an even crumb, add the oats and stir through. Then, stir in the spices and set aside.

Make the mushy peas. Place a saucepan on a medium heat and add the butter. Once the butter is melted, add the peas, ginger and chilli, then sweat down for about 5 minutes to soften. Add the garlic powder, garam masala and curry powder and leave to cook for a few minutes.

While the peas are cooking down, finish preparing the fish. Tip the flour on to a plate, place the beaten egg into a bowl and tip the spiced, pickled-onion crunchy coating on to another plate. One at a time, dip the fish fillets into the flour, then the egg and finally coat them in the crunchy coating.

Add a good splash of oil to a frying pan along with the butter, over a medium heat. Once foaming, carefully lay in the coated fish and fry for 3–4 minutes, until the underside coating is toasty golden brown. Then flip over the fillets and repeat on the other side.

While the fish is cooking, toast the muffin halves.

Once the fish fillets are cooked, add a little lemon juice to the pan and baste the butter and lemon juice over the fish. Lift the fish out of the fat and rest them on some kitchen paper set on a plate for a minute or so.

While the fish is resting, finish off the mushy peas. Cut the avocado in half and remove the stone. Scoop out the flesh with a spoon, add this to the mushy peas and crush everything together with a fork. Stir through the mint and set aside.

To serve, mix together the hot sauce and the mayonnaise in a bowl and spread the spiced mayo on to the base and lid of the toasted muffins. Divide the mushy peas between the muffin bases and top with the crispy-coated fish and finally the muffin lid. Tuck in!

Selin Kiazim

HALLOUMI LOAF

This is such an easy loaf to make and it's great to have in hunks for breakfast or as a snack with a cup of tea. It proved a firm favourite for us at home during lockdown. You could use a mixture of olives and halloumi, or just straight olives, if you prefer – just pit them and roughly chop before adding to the mixture.

Serves 4–6

500g plain flour
7g sachet of fast-action dried yeast
½ teaspoon fine salt
½ teaspoon caster sugar
125ml extra-virgin olive oil
½ onion, finely chopped
2 x 225g blocks of halloumi, cut into 1cm cubes
1 tablespoon dried mint

In a large bowl mix together the flour, yeast, salt and sugar. Add 400ml of water and half the olive oil to form a thick batter.

Add the onion, halloumi and dried mint and mix well.

Use the remaining olive oil to heavily grease a 900g loaf tin. Place the mixture into the tin and spread it out evenly. Cover with a damp cloth and leave it to rise in a warm place for about 2–3 hours, until doubled in size.

Preheat the oven to 210°C/190°C fan/Gas mark 6–7.

Place the risen loaf, in the tin, in the oven for 35 minutes, or until golden brown and a lovely crust has formed. A skewer inserted into the centre should come out clean. Leave to cool in the tin for 10 minutes, then turn out on to a wire rack to cool completely, before cutting into portions.

James Martin

CHEESE & TOMATO QUICHE

Get your bake on with this beautiful quiche, then serve it with a fresh green salad. It's a perfect lunchtime bite!

Serves 6–8

For the filling
5 tomatoes, halved
1 onion, sliced, then cooked in a knob of butter until caramelised
300g cheddar, grated
a few thyme sprigs, leaves picked

For the pastry
400g plain flour
200g unsalted butter, cubed and chilled, plus extra for greasing
1 pinch of salt
a few thyme sprigs, leaves picked (optional)
1 egg

For the custard
5 eggs
3 egg yolks
200ml double cream
200ml whole milk
salt and freshly ground black pepper

To serve
50ml vegetable oil
15ml white wine vinegar
1 tablespoon Dijon mustard
mixed green salad leaves

Preheat the oven to 120°C/100°C fan/Gas mark ½–1. First, prepare the tomatoes. Spread them out, cut sides up, on a baking tray and bake for 1 hour. Remove from the oven and set aside to cool. (Turn the oven off.)

Next, prepare the pastry. Place the flour into a bowl and add the butter and salt, and the thyme (if using). Rub the mixture between your fingers, until it looks like coarse breadcrumbs. Add the egg and mix with your fingertips to form a dough. Add a little water if needed, to help it come together. Tip out the dough on to a floured surface and knead until smooth, then wrap it in cling film and chill for 30 minutes.

Preheat the oven to 190°C/170°C fan/Gas mark 5. Grease a 27cm loose-bottomed tart tin and roll the pastry out on a lightly floured surface to the thickness of a £1 coin, and use to line the tin, with overhang to trim after baking. Line the pastry case with a piece of scrunched-up baking paper and fill it with baking beans. Blind bake the pastry case for 15–20 minutes, then remove the baking beans and paper and return the case to the oven for a further 5–10 minutes, until golden. Remove the pastry case from the oven and set aside. Reduce the oven to 160°C/140°C fan/Gas mark 2–3.

To make the custard, whisk together the eggs, egg yolks, cream and milk, then season with salt and pepper.

Spread the onion and baked tomatoes evenly over the pastry base. Pour the custard over the top, sprinkle in the cheese and thyme leaves and bake for 30–40 minutes, until the crust is golden and the filling is set with a slight wobble in the middle.

Meanwhile, prepare the salad to serve. Mix the oil, vinegar and mustard together to make a dressing and season to taste. Place the salad leaves in a bowl and pour over a little of the dressing.

Once the quiche is baked, let it sit for 5 minutes in the tin. Trim the edge of the pastry crust to neaten, then remove from the tin and serve hot, warm or cold with the salad and extra dressing on the side.

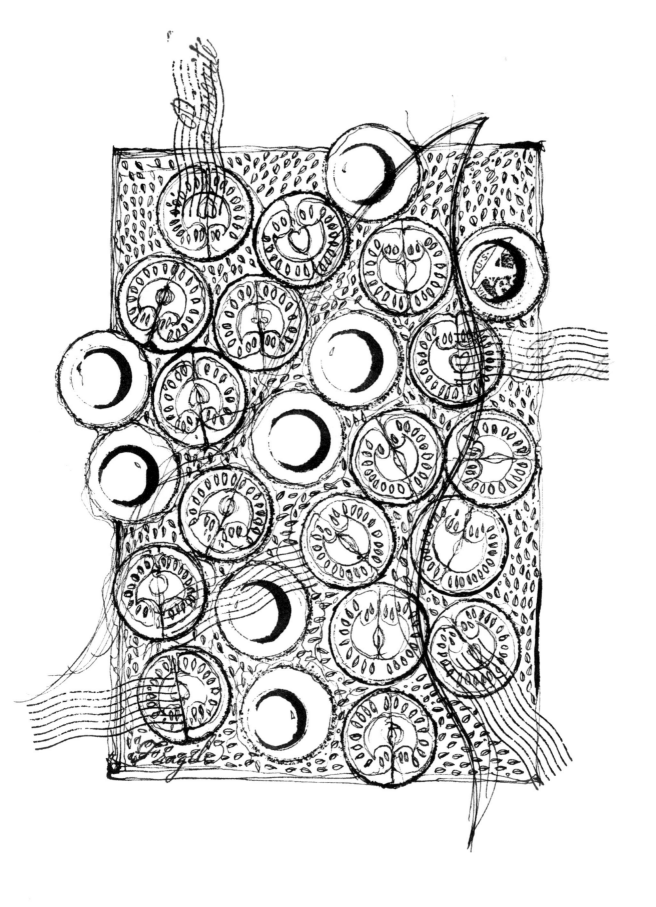

MASALA ROTI
with turmeric & chilli scrambled eggs

Spicy scrambled eggs have got to be my go-to meal no matter what time of day or night it is. Versatile, inexpensive and nutritious, scramble can go in a wrap, in a sandwich, inside a tea cake or simply on toast – or, if you've got more time, on homemade masala roti (Rajasthani spiced flat breads).

Serves 4

For the pickled shallots
250ml white wine or champagne vinegar
1 tablespoon caster sugar
2 shallots, thinly sliced

For the masala roti
250g chickpea flour
250g plain flour
1 teaspoon salt
2.5cm fresh ginger root, peeled and
   finely chopped
2 green chillies, finely chopped
2 tablespoons finely chopped coriander
1 teaspoon carom seeds (ajowan)
1 teaspoon black onion seeds (nigella seeds)
½ teaspoon red chilli powder
½ teaspoon ground turmeric
1 spring onion, finely chopped
2 tablespoons vegetable oil
3 tablespoons ghee or unsalted butter,
   for brushing

For the scrambled eggs
4 tablespoons vegetable or mustard oil
2 red onions, finely chopped
3 green chillies, finely chopped
1 teaspoon red chilli flakes
1 teaspoon ground turmeric
2 teaspoons salt
12 eggs, lightly beaten
2 tablespoons chopped coriander

First, make the pickled shallots. Put the vinegar and sugar in a pan with 125ml of water and bring to the boil. Remove from the heat and add the shallots. Allow to cool, then refrigerate. Leave the onions in the pickling liquor overnight if you can, or for at least 2–3 hours.

Make the masala roti. Combine the flours in a bowl, then remove 3–4 tablespoons and set aside for dusting at a later stage. Add the salt, ginger, green chillies, coriander, carom seeds, black onion seeds, red chilli powder, turmeric and spring onion and mix well. Add the oil and 225ml of water and knead to a stiff dough. If the dough feels slightly soft, add more flour and knead as necessary. Cover the dough with a damp tea towel and set aside for 5–10 minutes to rest.

Divide the rested dough into 8 equal pieces and shape each into a ball. Dust your work surface with some of the flour you set aside earlier, and, using a rolling pin, roll out the balls into circles, each about 15–20cm in diameter.

Heat a large frying pan over a high heat. Add a circle of the dough and cook on a dry heat for 3–4 minutes, until the dough starts to dry out and get some colour. Flip over the flat bread and cook on the other side. When both the sides are done, brush the flat bread with some ghee and turn it over again, repeating on the other side. Remove the roti from the pan and keep warm under a clean tea towel until you're ready to serve. Repeat for the other circles of dough.

Make the scrambled eggs. Heat the oil in a wok over a high heat. Add the onions and fry for 3–4 minutes, then add the green chillies and red chilli flakes and stir for 30 seconds or so, then add the turmeric and salt. Stir to mix, then add the beaten eggs.

Stir and scrape the eggs from the bottom of the wok, so that they scramble without sticking. Sprinkle with chopped coriander, check the seasoning and remove from the heat.

Divide the eggs into 4 equal portions, scatter with some of the drained pickled shallots and serve with the masala roti.

Robin Gill

MY IRISH ONION SOUP

If you have lots of onions in the pantry, my Irish onion soup is the perfect home for them. Warming and reassuring, this soup is best served with chunky sourdough, Branston pickle and cheese. Pint of Guinness optional.

Serves 3–4

300ml Guinness
125g unsalted butter
2kg onions (or a mixture of shallots and white and red onions), thinly sliced
4 garlic cloves, thinly sliced
splash of Worcestershire sauce, plus optional extra to serve
splash of sherry
2 bay leaves
1 litre chicken or vegetable stock
good pinch of salt and a generous pinch of white pepper

To serve
3–4 large slices of 3-day-old sourdough, halved
1 tablespoon Branston pickle
150g Gruyère or good cheddar, grated

First, place the Guinness in a small pan over a medium–high heat and bring to the boil. Allow to bubble away until reduced by one third, then set aside.

Place a wide-bottomed pan over a medium–high heat. Add the butter and, once melted and foaming, add the onions and garlic. Add a good pinch of salt (this helps extract the moisture from the onions) and stir, then cover with a lid and cook for 10 minutes, removing the lid to stir every now and then, until the onions are soft. After 10 minutes, remove the lid and turn down the heat to low.

Continue to cook the onions and garlic, using a flat-ended wooden spoon to scrape the caramelised areas from the bottom of the pan, for up to 1 hour, until you get a lovely dark, golden-brown colour on the onions. Take the pan off the heat from time to time, using the steam to help deglaze the pan – this is where all the flavour is.

When you're happy with your onions, add the splashes of Worcestershire sauce and sherry, along with the bay leaves and reduced Guinness. Cook for 5 minutes, then add the stock and simmer for 30 minutes, until thick, but still with a soup consistency. Season to taste.

When you're ready to serve, heat the grill to high and toast the sliced sourdough on both sides, until golden and crunchy. Remove from the grill, but leave the grill on.

Pour the soup into heatproof serving bowls, spread the Branston pickle on each toast and float two slices on top of each portion of soup. Cover the toasts with the grated cheese, then place the bowls under the grill, until the cheese melts, bubbles and browns. I add a little more Worcestershire sauce to mine, then serve.

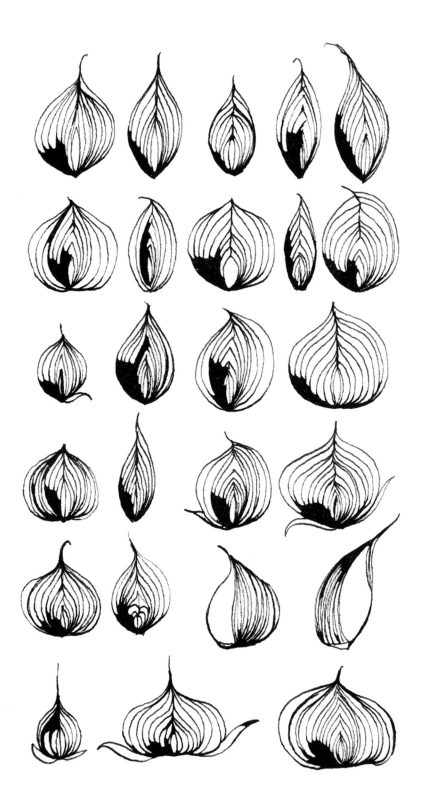

Michael Caines

PUMPKIN SOUP

This is a great autumn or winter warmer. A simple and delicious recipe that makes the most of what can be an underrated ingredient in the form of the pumpkin. My preference is to use crown prince pumpkin which has a slightly better texture. Roasting and baking in the oven intensifies the flavour, bringing depth to the dish. My favourite way to serve is in a mug in front of the wood fire on the colder days of the year.

Serves 3–4

1kg crown prince pumpkin
50ml olive oil
50g unsalted butter
1 onion, sliced
2 garlic cloves, chopped
750ml light chicken stock
1 bouquet garni (parsley stalks, thyme, bay, leek and celery)
50ml double cream
salt and freshly ground black pepper

To garnish
5 tablespoons pumpkin seeds (from the pumpkin)
pumpkin seed oil

Preheat the oven to 180°C/160°C fan/Gas mark 4.

Halve the pumpkin, remove the seeds, discarding the stringy bits, then washing and drying them and reserving them for the garnish. Cut the pumpkin flesh (skin on) into large segments. Drizzle the oil over a baking tray and add the pumpkin pieces. Transfer to the oven and bake for 45 minutes, until dried out. Remove the pumpkin from the oven and leave to cool, then scrape out the flesh, discarding the skins.

Melt the butter in a saucepan over a medium heat. Add the onion, garlic and a little salt and sauté for about 10–12 minutes, until soft, but not taking on any colour.

Add the roasted pumpkin, along with the chicken stock, bouquet garni and a little more salt. Pour in 750ml of water and bring to the boil, then reduce to a simmer and cook for 20 minutes. Leave to stand for 10 minutes.

Meanwhile, toast the pumpkin seeds in a dry frying pan over a low–medium heat for about 2 minutes, until lightly coloured. Set aside until you're ready to serve.

Remove the bouquet garni from the soup and ladle the soup into a blender – be careful not to overfill. Blend until smooth, then pass the soup through a fine sieve back into the saucepan. Add the cream and bring back to the boil. Season with salt and pepper.

Ladle the soup into bowls, then sprinkle with the toasted pumpkin seeds. Finish with a swirl of pumpkin seed oil.

Chef's notes...

This soup works beautifully well with carrots too – just swap like for like in terms of weight, but roast the carrots for a little less time than the pumpkin.

CHILLED GARDEN SOUP
with smoked salmon and crème fraîche

All the ingredients for this chilled soup are raw, so you'll need a strong blender to break them down. I use a slim blender (such as a Nutribullet) for the smoothest results, although a food processor is also good. The soup will keep in the fridge for a couple of days, so you can prepare it in advance.

Serves 4

150g frozen peas
½ large cucumber, skin on, cut into chunks
60g pickled gherkins, roughly chopped if
   you wish
200g stale bread, crusts removed, torn
   into pieces
2 courgettes, grated
handful of curly parsley, chopped
½ bunch of dill
250g green lettuce, such as cos or iceberg,
   roughly chopped
150g crème fraîche, plus extra to finish
50ml good olive oil, plus extra to finish
10 ice cubes
salt and freshly ground black pepper
smoked salmon, torn into thin strips,
   to serve

Put the peas, cucumber and gherkins into the blender and whizz until smooth. Pass the mixture through a fine sieve into a bowl to remove any remaining lumps.

Add the pieces of torn bread and leave the mixture for a few minutes until the bread is fully soaked.

Meanwhile, put the courgettes, parsley, dill, lettuce, crème fraîche, olive oil and ice cubes into the blender. Add the liquid/bread mixture, season well, and whizz until smooth. Check the seasoning and adjust as necessary.

To serve, divide the soup equally among 4 wide bowls. Dress the top of each bowl with the salmon strips, almost piled in the centre, and top with a little crème fraîche. Finally, drizzle with olive oil and finish with a grinding of pepper.

LYONNAISE ONION SOUP

A Roux household favourite, this is a filling soup – a delicious classic that is traditionally devoured after getting home very late from a night out. It's invigorating, warming and totally satisfying. Adding crème fraîche or cream, port and egg yolks is typical of the Lyon region. They add richness and depth of flavour. One variation, which my father liked, is to replace the white wine with dry cider and the port with Calvados. The soup then becomes 'à la Normande'.

Serves 4–6

120g unsalted butter
2 tablespoons vegetable oil
1kg best-quality onions, sliced
1 tablespoon thyme leaves
1 bottle of dry white wine
60g plain flour
1.8 litres beef stock
5 egg yolks
100ml port
250g crème fraîche
4–6 slices of baguette
300g Gruyère cheese
salt and freshly ground black pepper

Melt 60g of the butter in a pan with the oil over a medium heat. Add the onions and cook over a low–medium heat, stirring occasionally, for about 30–40 minutes, until the onions caramelise and become sweet and tender – don't cover the pan. Add the thyme and white wine, increase the heat to medium, and cook until reduced by half.

Melt the remaining 60g of butter in a pan. Add the flour and mix well to make a roux. Cook until a light brown colour, but take care not to let the mixture burn. Pour in the beef stock, whisking well to combine, then simmer for 5 minutes. Add this mixture to the onions, season well and cook for a further 30 minutes, until thickened.

Preheat the grill to high.

Mix the egg yolks, port and crème fraîche together and divide the mixture equally between 4–6 soup bowls. Ladle in the piping-hot soup, stirring it into the egg mixture with a fork as you do so.

Generously sprinkle the baguette slices with the cheese, then place the croûtons on to a grill pan and grill for about 3 minutes, until the cheese is golden and bubbling. Place one croûton on top of each serving of soup and serve immediately.

Naved Nasir

CHILLI BROCCOLI SALAD

Toasted pistachios and shredded mint leaves with broccoli, fresh red chillies, pumpkin seeds, dates and honey, all dressed up in lime and chilli – this is a most delicious lunch, or a welcome addition to your Sunday table (at Dishoom we suggest serving it alongside lamb raan and naan).

This dressing makes more than you need, but the extra will keep in the fridge for 3–4 days and works brilliantly on any salad or green vegetables, and is also delicious drizzled over ripe avocado, or served with grilled fish.

Serves 2 *as a side or 1 as a main*

140–150g broccoli, blanched then chopped
   into pieces no larger than 1cm
60g roasted pistachio nuts, lightly crushed
½ red chilli, finely chopped
4–5 coriander sprigs, torn
5–6 mint leaves, torn
20g Medjool dates, finely chopped
10g runny honey
20g roasted pumpkin seeds
1 lime, cut into wedges
salt

For the lime and chilli dressing
1½ tablespoons lime juice
3–4 thin slices of ginger
1 small green chilli
¼ teaspoon fine sea salt
1 tablespoon granulated sugar
2 teaspoons rice vinegar
60ml mild olive oil
a few mint leaves

First prepare the dressing. Using a mini processor or hand-held stick blender, blitz all the dressing ingredients until completely homogenised. Refrigerate until needed.

Combine the broccoli, pistachios, chilli, coriander, mint, dates, and a little salt to taste, in a bowl and toss together. Dress with about 2–3 tablespoons of the lime and chilli dressing, then drizzle with the honey and sprinkle with the pumpkin seeds. Give the salad a squeeze of lime to taste and serve with a lime wedge to garnish.

Giorgio Locatelli

PAN-FRIED CAULIFLOWER SALAD

This recipe adds the wow-factor to the humble cauliflower and is a unique take on the unassuming salad. The dressing is one of my favourites and can be used to bring countless other dishes to life.

Serves 6

2 cauliflower heads, separated into florets
olive oil, for frying
3 hard-boiled eggs, chopped
15 black olives, pitted
1 tablespoon capers in vinegar, drained
  and rinsed
1 teaspoon chopped mild red chilli
1 tablespoon chopped flat-leaf parsley
sea salt and freshly ground black pepper

For the dressing
½ teaspoon sea salt
3 tablespoons red wine vinegar
2 tablespoons white wine vinegar
300ml extra-virgin olive oil, preferably a fruity
  southern Italian one

First, prepare the dressing. Put the salt into a bowl. Add the vinegars and leave for 1 minute to allow the salt to dissolve. Whisk in the olive oil with 2 tablespoons of water, until the liquids emulsify. Set aside until needed.

Blanch the cauliflower in salted boiling water for 2 minutes – the florets should still be crunchy – then drain.

Heat a little olive oil in a pan over a medium–high heat, add the cauliflower and sauté for about 5–7 minutes, until golden all over. Transfer to a large serving bowl.

Add the eggs, olives, capers, chilli and parsley to the serving bowl. Drizzle in 200ml of the dressing, mix everything together very gently so that you don't break up the egg yolks any further, then season to taste and serve.

Chef's notes...

Store any remaining dressing in a clean squeezy bottle and keep it in the fridge for up to a month. It will separate out, so just give it a good shake before you use it.

John Williams

MY HOME NIÇOISE SALAD

This salad is something that I resort to regularly. Whenever I want something tasty and rewarding with wonderful flavours, this is where I end up. Throughout lockdown, on those warm, sunny days, I enjoyed this with my children and a lovely glass of white wine. The recipe benefits from some of the most delicious ingredients: new potatoes, olives and basil. Get those right and you simply can't go far wrong.

Serves 4

100g new potatoes, I use Jersey potatoes
3 eggs
60g French beans or extra fine beans
60g broad beans
6 cherry tomatoes, halved
25ml Cabernet Sauvignon vinegar (or any other good-quality red wine vinegar)
75ml good-quality extra-virgin olive oil
2 lettuce hearts, leaves separated
2 cos lettuce, leaves separated
12 pitted black olives
12 pitted green olives
1 large shallot, thinly sliced
¼ cucumber, cut into 2cm-thick chunks
180g tinned tuna steak in olive oil, drained
3 baby artichokes (preserved are good), quartered
24 basil leaves
sea salt flakes and freshly ground black pepper

Bring a pan of salted water to the boil over a high heat and add the new potatoes. Cook for about 15 minutes, until tender, then drain and when cool enough to handle, remove the skins and slice the flesh into thick roundels. Set aside at room temperature (do not refrigerate).

Meanwhile, cook the eggs for 6 minutes, until just hard boiled. Drain, leave to cool, then remove the shells and cut each egg into quarters.

Bring two pans of water to the boil. Add the broad beans to one and the French beans to the other. Gently boil for 3–4 minutes, until the beans are tender. Drain, then immediately refresh in iced water and drain again. Cut the French beans into pieces 4cm long and set aside.

Season the tomato halves with salt. Set aside.

Mix the vinegar and oil together in a small bowl to create a dressing and season to taste. Place all the lettuce leaves in a large serving bowl and sprinkle over about one third of the dressing.

Place the cooked potatoes and beans, both olives, and the tomatoes, shallot, cucumber, tuna and artichokes in a large bowl. Pour over the remaining dressing and mix in the basil leaves. Place the mixture on top of the dressed lettuce, top with the quartered boiled eggs, and serve.

Chef's notes...

This is much better when nothing has been refrigerated!

Saiphin Moore

SPICY BEEF SALAD

During lockdown it was harder to get authentic Thai ingredients, so I was making recipes with things I already had in the kitchen. Spicy beef salad is a super simple dish to make, and it doesn't use any hard-to-find ingredients. All you need to do is grill the meat and make a salad dressing. It's super healthy which was important for us during lockdown, to make sure the food we ate made us feel good. It's got all the flavours of Thai food – salty, sweet, sour and spicy!

Serves 4

300g beef sirloin or tenderloin
1 red onion, thinly sliced
½ cucumber, halved lengthways and sliced
   into half moons
8 cherry tomatoes, halved
60g mixed salad leaves

For the dressing
10 small garlic cloves
5 bird's eyes chillies (deseeded if you want
   less heat)
3 tablespoons fish sauce
3 tablespoons fresh lime juice
2 tablespoons chilli sauce (sriracha)
1 tablespoon palm sugar (or white
   granulated sugar)

To serve
handful of coriander leaves
2 spring onions, white parts only,
   finely chopped
Thai parsley (optional)

Prepare the dressing. Pound the garlic and chillies together in a pestle and mortar or blitz them in a food processor. Scoop the mixture into a dish and add the fish sauce, lime juice, chilli sauce and sugar. Stir until the sugar dissolves and set aside.

Preheat a non-stick griddle pan, wipe the beef dry and cut it into 2.5cm-thick steaks. Cook over a medium–high heat for no more than 2 minutes on each side, or until the meat is cooked to your liking. Slice thinly.

In a mixing bowl combine the cooked beef, onion, cucumber and tomatoes. Pour the dressing over and add the salad leaves. Toss to combine.

Transfer to serving bowls and garnish with coriander, spring onion, and Thai parsley (if using).

ASPARAGUS & POACHED EGGS
with mustard dressing

I look forward to having this dish every year – it is a celebration of the first British asparagus, cooked simply. What a treat.

Serves 4

For the mustard dressing
1 tablespoon Dijon mustard
1 tablespoon white wine vinegar
3 tablespoons groundnut or other
   non-scented oil
pinch of sea salt
2 turns of freshly ground black pepper

For the asparagus and spinach
225g (16 spears) green asparagus, trimmed
30g unsalted butter
150g spinach, leaves picked and washed
sea salt and freshly ground black pepper

For the poached eggs
2 teaspoons white wine vinegar
4 eggs

To finish
4 tablespoons hazelnuts, toasted in a
   180°C/160°C fan/Gas mark 4 oven for
   8 minutes, then roughly chopped

Prepare the mustard dressing. Mix all of the dressing ingredients together with 2 tablespoons of water, then taste and adjust the seasoning if necessary. Place in a large bowl ready to dress the asparagus.

In a medium saucepan, bring 1 litre of water to the boil with a pinch of salt. Add the asparagus and cook for 2 minutes, until al dente. Remove from the water, toss in the mustard dressing and keep warm.

Heat the butter in a large pan and sauté the spinach for 1 minute, until wilted.

Next, prepare the eggs. Pour 1 litre of water into a medium saucepan and place over a high heat. Add a little salt and the vinegar and bring to the boil.

Crack each egg into its own individual small bowl. Carefully stir the boiling water with a spoon to create a small whirlpool. Gently tip each egg from its bowl into the centre of the swirling water. Turn the heat down to medium, so the water is simmering, and cook the eggs for 3–4 minutes, until the whites are cooked but the yolks are runny.

Using a slotted spoon, remove the eggs one at a time and drain them on a tray lined with kitchen paper. Season with sea salt and freshly ground black pepper.

To serve, arrange 4 spears of asparagus on each plate, lining them up next to each other. Arrange the spinach on top of the asparagus to form a nest for the egg, and place the egg inside. Spoon the remaining mustard dressing around the plate and sprinkle the toasted hazelnuts over the egg and around the plate. Finish with a little black pepper to serve.

Thomasina Miers

MEAT-FREE CHILLI
with roast roots & beans

This recipe was born out of a love for the warming flavours of great chilli con carne but not always wanting to eat a big bowl of meat. I challenged myself to make a chilli using only delicious autumnal root veg. Here it is, a wonderfully aromatic result that can work for a party, with salsas, slaw, guac, tortilla chips and jacket potatoes, quinoa or rice, or for a mid-week dinner.

Wahaca staff cooked this for Chefs in Schools' children's hampers throughout lockdown. It's a recipe that I associate with a time when, even though the restaurant doors were closed, we were able to support our community.

Serves 6–8

700g crown prince or butternut squash, peeled, deseeded and cut into 3–4cm chunks
500g parsnips, peeled and cut into 3–4cm chunks
6 tablespoons olive or rapeseed oil
2 chipotle chillies, deseeded and opened like a book
1 ancho chilli, deseeded and opened like a book
boiling water
2 onions, chopped
4 garlic cloves, roughly chopped
2 teaspoons ground cumin
1 teaspoon ground coriander
1 teaspoon ground cinnamon
1 teaspoon dried oregano, preferably Mexican
2 x 400g tins of black beans, or a more locally grown bean from Hodmedod's, rinsed
2 x 400g tins of plum tomatoes
1–2 tablespoons light brown soft sugar, to taste
30g 70% dark chocolate, grated
salt and freshly ground black pepper

To serve
small bunch of coriander, leaves picked
guacamole
soured cream
jacket potatoes, or cooked quinoa or rice

Preheat the oven to 220°C/200°C fan/Gas mark 7.

Put the squash and parsnips on a baking tray. Drizzle over half the oil and season generously. Toss everything together with your hands, spread the mixture out and roast for 30–35 minutes, until the veg are tender but crisp and golden on the edges.

Toast the dried chillies in a small, dry frying pan over a medium heat, for 1 minute on both sides, then transfer to a heatproof bowl, cover with boiling water and set aside.

Meanwhile, pour the remaining oil into a large saucepan. Add the onions and sweat over a medium heat for 10 minutes, until the onions begin to soften. Season generously, add the garlic and cook for another 5–7 minutes. Drain the dried chillies, finely chop with a knife and add half to the onions with the spices and oregano. Fry for 1 minute, then add the beans, tomatoes, sugar and chocolate. Fill the tomato tin with hot water and add that too.

Bring the liquid to the boil and simmer for 15 minutes to allow the flavours to get to know one another. Stir in the roasted vegetables and check the seasoning. If you like a bit more heat, add the rest of the chillies. Simmer for another 15 minutes, until the sauce has thickened.

Check the seasoning, then sprinkle over the coriander leaves and serve with guacamole, soured cream and potatoes, quinoa or rice.

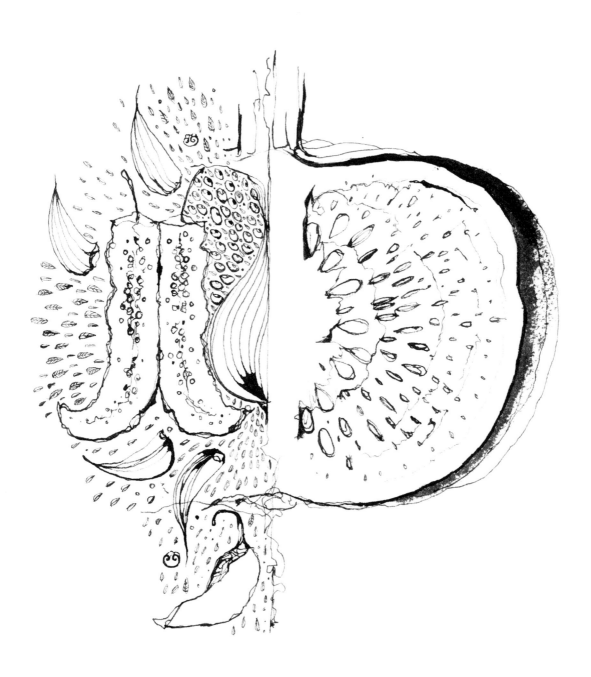

Chantelle Nicholson

ROASTED AUBERGINE
with harissa & sesame

This is a rich and comforting dish with the nuttiness of the sesame shining through. I love to add a big handful of chopped coriander, but I know that isn't to everyone's taste, so parsley works well as an alternative. Try serving the dish with roasted potatoes, cooked grains or a green vegetable salad.

Serves 2–4

2 aubergines, each cut into 6 wedges
4 tablespoons olive oil
2 tablespoons harissa paste
4 tablespoons tahini
juice and finely grated zest of
    ½ unwaxed lemon
2 tablespoons sesame seeds, toasted
½ bunch of coriander or flat-leaf
    parsley, chopped
salt

Preheat the oven to 200°/180°C fan/Gas mark 6.

Brush the aubergine wedges liberally with the olive oil and sprinkle generously with salt. Place in a roasting dish or baking tray and bake for 10 minutes, then brush with the harissa and return to the oven for a further 10 minutes, until coloured and cooked through.

Meanwhile, mix the tahini with 4 tablespoons of water and the lemon juice and zest. Season to taste with salt.

When the aubergine is cooked, sprinkle over the toasted sesame seeds. Transfer to a serving dish and drizzle over the tahini dressing. Finish with a scattered handful of chopped herbs.

GRILLED COURGETTES
with parsnip purée & rocket pesto

You can generally find courgettes in a range of different shapes and colours at food markets these days. Along with others, I like to use trompetta in my mixture – these are long, pale and somewhat curly, and have fewer seeds than regular courgettes. Grilling courgettes is one of the easiest ways to cook them, as there's hardly any prep – you just wash, slice and grill and they're utterly delicious.

Serves 4–6

1kg mixed courgettes (round, yellow
   and trompetta)
40ml extra-virgin olive oil, plus extra
   for drizzling
pinch of smoked paprika
5 walnuts, grated
sea salt and freshly ground black pepper

For the parsnip purée
400g parsnips, peeled and cut into small cubes
500ml double cream
30g unsalted butter
50ml extra-virgin olive oil
1 bay leaf

For the pesto
4 bunches of basil, leaves picked
1 garlic clove, crushed
200g pine nuts
200ml extra-virgin olive oil
250g manchego (or other hard sheep's
   cheese), cut into rough chunks

First, make the purée. Put the parsnips into a pan with the double cream, butter, olive oil and bay leaf. Season with salt and pepper and simmer until the parsnips are very soft. Remove from the heat and use a hand-held blender to blitz until nice and creamy. Taste for seasoning and adjust if necessary, then return the pan to a low heat, cover and keep warm until you're ready to serve.

Make the pesto. Blitz together the basil, garlic, pine nuts and olive oil to make a smooth-ish green paste. Add the manchego and pulse so that you have little chunks of cheese throughout, then season to taste, and mix well.

Cook the courgettes just before you're ready to eat. Trim them, slice them in half lengthways, then halve them again widthways. If you have round courgettes, cut them into wedges of a similar size. Put the courgettes into a bowl and season with the olive oil, and salt and pepper.

Heat a barbecue grill or a frying pan until hot.

Grill the courgettes, turning as necessary, until they are caramelised on both sides. (If you're using a pan, carefully place each slice in the pan and turn the slices when they are coloured but still with a bite to them.) When they are caramelised on both sides, remove to a tray or plate and drizzle with olive oil.

To serve, spoon the warm parsnip purée on to serving plates, top with the grilled courgettes, then dot over the pesto. Gently sprinkle over the smoked paprika, and finish with more olive oil and the grated walnuts.

Claude Bosi

CORNISH CRAB QUICHE

Some key ingredients, such as flour, were hard to source early on during lockdown, so I started making this delicious quiche with ready-made pastry, getting round that flour shortage as well as making it less time consuming to make at home.

Cornwall can rightfully boast that it supplies the best of a lot of produce, particularly seafood, and Cornish crab is one of my favourites.

Serves 16

1 x 500g block of shortcrust pastry
drizzle of olive oil
3 large leeks, thinly sliced
knob of salted butter
3 eggs
400ml double cream
200ml whole milk
6 egg yolks
170g brown crab meat
salt and freshly ground black pepper

To serve
white crab meat
zest of 1 lemon
1 teaspoon snipped chives
1 teaspoon salted butter, softened
crème fraîche

Preheat the oven to 170°C/150°C fan/Gas mark 3.

Roll out the pastry on a lightly floured surface to a circle the thickness of a £1 and use it to line a greased, 30cm quiche dish or tin, leaving the excess to come slightly up above the rim. Line the pastry case with baking paper and fill it with baking beans, then transfer it to the oven to bake for 25 minutes, until lightly golden.

While the pastry is baking, prepare a leek fondue mixture. Heat a frying pan over a medium heat and add the oil. When hot, add the leeks and the butter. Season well, cover with a lid and braise the leeks gently on a low heat for 25–30 minutes, until softened and caramelised. Check for seasoning, adding salt and pepper to taste if needed.

Once the pastry has been blind baking for 25 minutes, remove it from the oven and take out the beans and baking paper. Beat 1 of the whole eggs and use it to lightly egg wash the pastry. Return the case to the oven for 5 more minutes, until golden. Set aside to cool and turn the oven down to 150°C/130°C fan/Gas mark 2.

In a bowl, mix together the cream, milk, egg yolks, brown crab meat and the remaining 2 whole eggs, seasoning with salt and pepper. Add the mixture to the leek fondue and stir well to combine.

Spoon the mixture into the pastry case, ensuring it is evenly spread out. Transfer the quiche to the oven and cook for 40 minutes, then increase the heat to 170°C/150°C fan/Gas mark 3 and bake for a further 20 minutes, until the filling is set with just a slight wobble in the centre, then remove from the oven.

While the quiche is baking, combine the white crab meat with the lemon zest, chives, and salted butter. Stir through a generous helping of crème fraîche, and season with pepper.

When the quiche is ready, serve warm with a spoonful of the dressed crab meat alongside.

Richard Corrigan

SHELLFISH COCKTAIL

The quantities for the seafood in this recipe are up to you and depend on your own preferences – just try to get a good mixture of everything, from crab meat to prawns and some lobster and shrimp too. Similarly, how much sauce you make is really up to you. To serve, I always think this looks best, and most traditional, in old-fashioned cocktail glasses.

Serves 4

mixture of seafood including picked white
    crab meat, Dublin Bay prawns, Atlantic
    prawns, cooked lobster tails and brown
    shrimps (peeled)
extra-virgin olive oil
squeeze of lemon juice
2 baby gem lettuce
1 avocado, stoned and finely diced
1 small cucumber, peeled, deseeded and diced
salt

For the cocktail sauce
2 parts mayonnaise
1 part tomato ketchup
splash of brandy
dash of Tabasco
pinch of paprika
splash of Worcestershire sauce
squeeze of lemon juice

Mix together all the ingredients for the sauce. Keep tasting it, and adjust it until it makes you smile, then set aside until ready to serve.

Season all the seafood with a little extra-virgin olive oil, salt and a drop of lemon juice.

To assemble, put some lettuce, avocado and cucumber at the bottom of the glasses, which will give a lovely crunch, then layer up your seafood, put a dollop of sauce on top and let people mix everything up, or keep everything separate, as they choose.

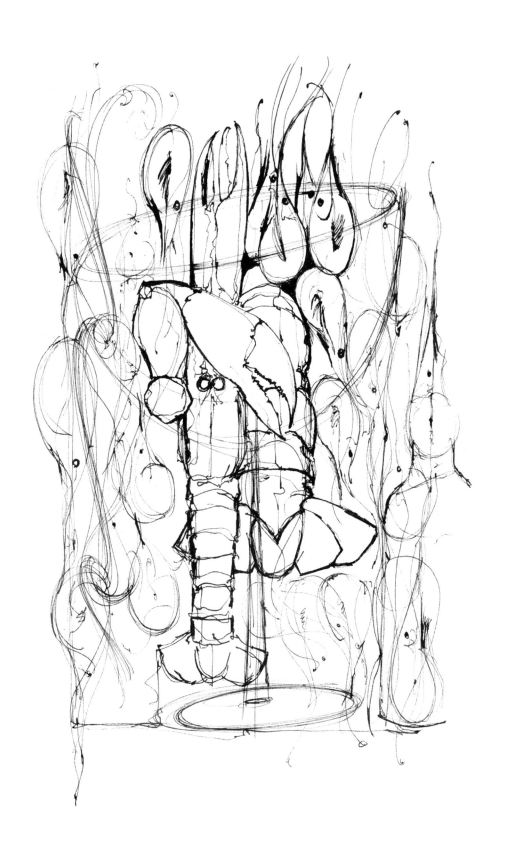

WHITE BEANS & MUSSELS
with wild fennel aioli

This was one of my easiest and favourite lockdown dishes. I had a whole load of fennel growing in a trough that definitely wasn't locked down! I made soup, mayonnaise, vinegar – I tried all sorts, but this garlicky, aniseed-flavour mayo came out tops. It turned out to be one of those dishes that we all loved, mostly because the first bit of fresh seafood we got our hands on was a bag of mussels from our bay. As ever, I kept it simple – I couldn't be bothered to queue at the shops, so with the mussels in hand, the only other ingredients I used were already in the cupboard. You could cheat, of course – it's still good using a tin of white beans and a jar of mayo – but if you want the best results, here's how I did it.

Serves 4

150g white beans, soaked overnight
150ml olive oil
½ onion, chopped
4 garlic cloves, crushed
1kg mussels in their shells, washed well
    and debearded
½ glass dry white wine
handful of curly parsley, finely chopped
toasted sourdough bread, or greens, to serve

For the mayo
1 tablespoon Dijon mustard
1 garlic clove, peeled
1 egg yolk
capful of Pernod or Ricard
200ml vegetable oil
handful of wild fennel, finely chopped
pinch each of salt and white pepper

Put the beans in a pan with enough water to cover and 100ml of the olive oil. Bring to a simmer and leave simmering for an hour or so, topping up with more water if needed, until the beans are giving and falling apart.

Heat the remaining olive oil in a large pan on a medium heat. Add the onions and the crushed garlic cloves and sweat for about 5 minutes, until soft. Add the mussels, then the wine, place the lid on the pan and steam for about 2 minutes, until all the mussels open. Allow to cool, then use a slotted spoon to remove the mussels from the liquid (discard any that stay shut). Take the mussel meat out of the shells and put it back in the liquid with the parsley, then add a few tablespoons of the beans until you have a nice balance between beans, mussels and juice – it's not a soup, more of a bean salad-type of dish. Set aside while you make the mayo.

In a food processor, mix together the mustard, garlic, egg yolk and Pernod or Ricard, then slowly add the oil in a thin stream, until the mixture is thick and creamy. Stir in the chopped fennel – you want it really green and tasting of garlic. Season to taste, then immediately serve with the mussels and the sourdough or greens.

Andrew Wong

YANGZHOU FRIED RICE

This is an easy midweek dinner that was so good to cook during lockdown. We added any leftover vegetables we could lay our hands on.

Serves 2

2 tablespoons vegetable oil
1 egg, lightly beaten
50g Char Siu roasted pork or pork
    tenderloin, diced
50g Chinese fish cake, diced
20g frozen peas, defrosted
400g cooked long-grain rice, chilled
4 tablespoons chopped spring onions (green
    parts only)
1 tablespoon sesame oil
salt and white pepper
soy or hot chilli sauce, to serve (optional)

Place a wok over a high heat. When hot, add the vegetable oil and allow to heat up. Add the egg and lightly scramble until it is 70 per cent cooked.

Throw in the pork, fish cake, peas and rice and mix well until everything is hot. Make sure that you keep an eye on the heat in order to prevent the mixture from catching on the bottom of the wok and turning your rice black.

Just before serving, season with salt and pepper, then add the spring onions and sesame oil. Serve with soy sauce or hot chilli sauce, if you wish.

Chef's notes...

For the best results, use day-old cooked rice or cook 200g of rice according to packet instructions before you begin.

Jason Atherton

KEZIAH'S RATATOUILLE

With its links to my life as a chef, Ratatouille is one of our family's favourite movies. Naturally, therefore, we like to cook our version, which the children love as it is full of bright, rainbow colours. This is a perfect accompaniment to a Sunday roast chicken, or just with plenty of bread to mop up the juices.

Serves 8

2 aubergines
6 Roma or plum tomatoes, sliced into
   5mm rounds
2 yellow courgettes, sliced into 5mm rounds
2 green courgettes, sliced into 5mm rounds
1 red onion, sliced into 5mm rounds

For the sauce
2 tablespoons olive oil
1 onion, diced
4 garlic cloves, crushed
2 tablespoons Chardonnay (or other
   good-quality white wine) vinegar
1 red pepper, deseeded and diced
3 tomatoes
2 x 400g tins of crushed or chopped tomatoes
2 tablespoons chopped basil leaves
   (8–10 leaves)
salt and freshly ground black pepper

For the herb dressing
2 tablespoons chopped basil leaves
   (8–10 leaves)
1 garlic clove, crushed
2 teaspoons thyme leaves
4 tablespoons olive oil

First, prepare the sauce. Heat the olive oil in a saucepan on a medium–low heat. Sweat the onions and garlic for 5–7 minutes, until soft, stirring to avoid any browning. Deglaze the pan with the vinegar, then add the pepper and tomatoes, and season to taste. (Seasoning at this point helps break down the vegetables.) When the pepper and tomatoes have softened, add the tinned tomatoes and stir through to combine. Cook on a low heat for 20–25 minutes, until thickened. Add the chopped basil and stir through.

Meanwhile, prepare the aubergines. One at a time, slice the smaller end until about a third of the way down. Cut the remaining piece in half lengthways and continue to slice into 5mm pieces.

Preheat the oven to 200°C/180°C fan/Gas mark 6.

Transfer the sauce into a circular ovenproof dish and spread it evenly over the base. Place the sliced vegetables into the sauce, alternating and slightly overlapping them in concentric circles, to completely cover the sauce.

Combine all the dressing ingredients in a small bowl and spoon this on top of the vegetables. Bake for 20 minutes, until hot and bubbling. Serve immediately.

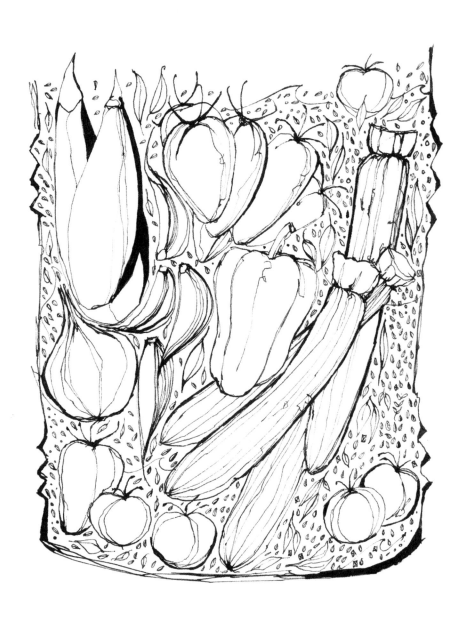

Jack Stein

LANGOUSTINE LINGUINE
with gochujang

This is a variation of a traditional crab linguine. I find the miso and the gochujang give a subtle back flavour that you don't get by adding chilli flakes. Langoustine meat is expensive, so you can of course substitute it for prawns or crab, depending on what is available.

Serves 4

450g dried linguine
50ml extra-virgin olive oil
1 garlic clove, finely chopped
300g langoustine meat, chopped
3 tomatoes, deseeded and chopped
½ teaspoon miso paste (light or dark is fine)
1 teaspoon gochujang paste
1 tablespoon chopped parsley
2 tablespoons lemon juice
sea salt and freshly ground black pepper

Cook the pasta in a large pan of well-salted, boiling water for 7 minutes, until tender.

Meanwhile, heat the olive oil in a large pan until hot. Add the garlic and sauté for 1 minute over a low heat. Then, add the chopped langoustine meat, tomatoes, miso and gochujang and cook for another 1 minute.

Drain the pasta, then transfer it to the pan with the sauce and briefly toss everything together. Finish with parsley and lemon juice, and season with salt and pepper.

Chef's notes...

To get the langoustine meat out from the shell, briefly boil the langoustines whole for 2–3 minutes, then cool and peel. Keep the shells and poach them in olive oil for 20 minutes to have great shellfish oil for the fridge.

Elizabeth Haigh

FRIED EGG & SAMBAL
with rice & soy sauce

Lockdown was really hard on our restaurant, Mei Mei, as we had been open only a few months. It was so important for us to be able to pivot really quickly to stay functioning. We made our signature sauces (such as kaya coconut jam and sambal) available to buy online, and we were overwhelmed with the amount of support we got in the first two weeks.

As my entire team was furloughed, it was up to me to produce, fulfil, distribute and manage all the orders. As well as that, I was cooking for the local neighbourhood's vulnerable, so I barely had a second during the lockdown to look after myself. The one thing that kept me going and helped me to stay positive was knowing that there will be an end to it.

For me, there's nothing more comforting than a simple runny egg over freshly steamed rice with a glug of soy sauce over the top. The sambal is a sambal tumis belachan, a spicy, shrimp-cooked chilli paste that goes with everything. It was the best-seller over the lockdown and continues to be my favourite sauce to make.

Serves 4

200g jasmine rice
1 pandan leaf, knotted (optional)
1 tablespoon rapeseed oil
4 eggs

To finish
dark soy sauce
ground white pepper
Mei Mei Sambal tumis belachan

In a large bowl, rinse the rice under cold running water until the water runs clear.

Place the rice into a saucepan with enough water to cover it and an extra 1cm depth. (If you place your index finger into the saucepan to touch the top of the rice, the water should come up to the first finger line.) Add the pandan leaf to the pan, if you're using it.

Bring the rice to the boil over a high heat and wait for the grains to start 'dancing', then reduce the heat to a gentle simmer. Don't be tempted to stir it. When the surface of the rice is almost dry, turn the heat off and cover with a lid for 10 minutes, until the rice is tender.

In the meantime, heat the oil in a frying pan or wok over a high heat and fry the eggs, one at a time, until they are crispy on the edges but the yolks are still runny.

Fluff up the rice, remove and discard the pandan leaf, if necessary, then serve the rice in a bowl, with the runny egg on top and sprinkled with a dash of soy sauce and ground white pepper. Add as much or as little sambal to the dish as you wish, depending on how spicy you want it.

Chef's notes...

If you can't get hold of our sambal sauce, you can make a variation at home. Blend together 4 fresh chillies, 4 dried chillies, 2 peeled garlic cloves, 2 peeled banana shallots, 1 tablespoon brown sugar and 1 lemongrass, and then fry slowly in a few tablespoons of oil, continuously stirring until it is a rich red colour.

James Cochran

BUTTERMILK CHICKEN WINGS

Fried chicken is one of my signature dishes and it became a favourite of Around the Cluck, the home delivery service I started during lockdown. When I'm making this at home, I like to brine the chicken to retain as much moisture and tenderness before coating and frying – it's well worth effort if you have time.

You should be able to pick up buttermilk in most supermarkets, but if you can't find it you can make your own substitute: stir 2 tablespoons of lemon juice into 500ml milk, leave to settle for 10 minutes and you're done.

Serves 4

For the brine
50g salt
1 litre water
2 garlic cloves, smashed
4–6 thyme sprigs

For the chicken
1kg chicken wings, jointed in half
500ml buttermilk
vegetable oil, for frying
plain flour, for coating
small handful of roasted peanuts, blended

For the coriander mayonnaise
½ bunch of coriander, roughly chopped, plus
    extra to garnish
100ml vegetable oil
1 egg yolk
½ teaspoon salt

For the fish-sauce caramel
250ml fish sauce
juice and zest of 1 lime
250g caster sugar
2 dried chillies

Make the brine a day before you intend to brine the chicken. Place all the ingredients in a saucepan and place over a high heat. Bring to the boil, then remove from the heat and leave to cool. Transfer to a lidded container and refrigerate overnight. The following day, place the chicken wings in a deep dish so that they fit snugly in a single layer. Pour over the chilled brine and leave for 4 hours.

Meanwhile, prepare the coriander mayonnaise. Roughly chop the coriander and put into the Thermomix with the vegetable oil. Set the Thermo to 90°C and blend for 10 minutes, then pass through a fine sieve and chill for 30 minutes. Put the egg yolk, salt and 1 tablespoon of water in the Thermomix and blend. Gradually add the coriander oil and check for consistency and seasoning, then chill until needed. If you don't have a Thermomix, whisk the egg and salt, then very slowly add the vegetable oil. Stir in the coriander.

Put all the ingredients for the fish-sauce caramel into a pan and place over a medium heat. Bring to a simmer and leave to reduce to a caramel consistency. Pass the sauce through a fine sieve into a bowl, then transfer it to a bowl until you're ready to serve.

Tip the brined wings into a colander and leave them to drain for 5 minutes. Pour the buttermilk into a bowl and add the drained chicken, then turn to coat.

Heat the oil in a deep-fat fryer or large high-sided pan to 165°C. You need to make sure the oil is deep enough to cover the chicken, but don't fill a pan more than two-thirds full.

While the oil is heating, coat the wings in the flour, then, once the oil is hot, add to the oil in batches and fry, turning, for 6 minutes, or until golden and the chicken is cooked through. Set each batch aside to drain on kitchen paper while you cook the next.

To serve, divide the fried chicken among 4 plates, scatter with the peanuts and extra coriander, then serve with the mayo and caramel on the side.

Selin Kiazim

FOUR CHEESE, GARLIC & SPRING ONION PIDE

Pides are actually really easy to make and offer great alternatives to pizza. This is one of the dishes that my customers craved during lockdown, so I did a few videos on how to make it at home. You can use whatever you like for the filling, so let your imagination run wild. For the best restaurant-baked experience, use a pizza stone if you have one. I love to serve the pides with a zingy chopped salad.

Makes 6

For the dough
about 360ml lukewarm water
7g sachet instant dried yeast
1 tablespoon extra-virgin olive oil
1 teaspoon caster sugar
625g strong white bread flour
½ teaspoon fine salt
plain flour, for dusting
30g unsalted butter, melted, for brushing

For the filling
150g ball of mozzarella, diced
150g parmesan, finely grated
150g strong cheddar, grated (or kaşar if you can find it)
150g feta, crumbled
1 bunch of spring onions, finely sliced
½ bunch of parsley, finely shredded
2 garlic cloves, finely grated

Make the pide dough. Combine 150ml of the water with the yeast, olive oil and sugar, and mix to dissolve the sugar.

Place the bread flour into a large bowl and make a well in the centre. Add the salt to one side of the flour and add the yeast mixture into the well. Using one hand, incorporate the liquid into the flour, gradually adding the rest of the water, until you have a dough that comes together but doesn't stick to your hands. Knead for approximately 5 minutes, or until smooth. Transfer the dough to a clean bowl, cover with a damp cloth and leave to rise for about 1½–2 hours, until doubled in size.

Meanwhile, combine all the filling ingredients in a bowl and set aside.

Preheat the oven to 220°C/200°C fan/Gas mark 7 (put your pizza stone or a large non-stick baking tray in to heat up). Divide the risen dough into 6 equal pieces, roll them into balls and cover them with a damp cloth.

One ball at a time, roll the dough on a lightly floured surface into a large oval shape, approximately 25cm by 15cm, and 3mm thick.

Place one-sixth of the cheese mixture along the centre of the oval, leaving a 2cm border around the edge. Fold over the edges of the dough, leaving the centre of the filling exposed. (You're looking to achieve a canoe shape with the dough.) Pinch the ends of the dough really well to avoid the 'canoe' unravelling while baking. Repeat the process with the remaining dough balls and filling.

If you're using a stone, bake the pides as you go along – as soon as each one is filled and shaped, place it on the stone and bake it for 15–20 minutes, or until deep golden brown at the edges. If you don't have a stone, you can place multiple pides on the large baking tray and bake in one go for 15–20 minutes, instead.

Brush the edges with melted butter and serve immediately.

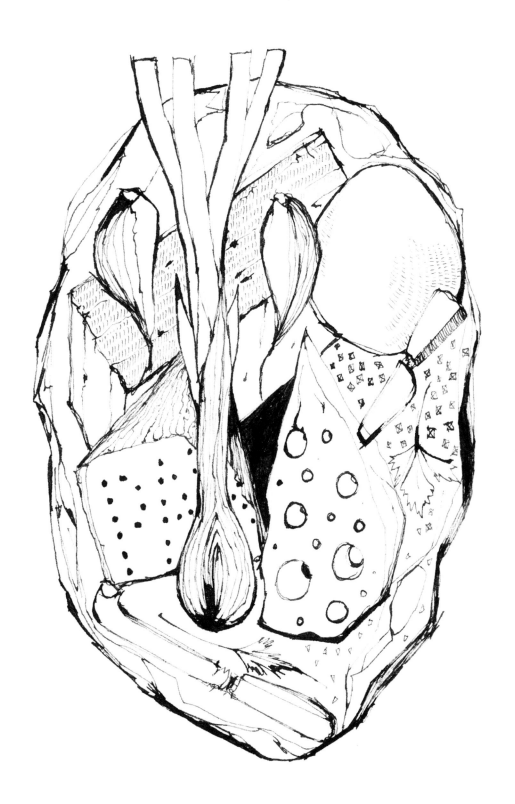

Vivek Singh

LENTIL & BASMATI KICHRI
with burnt aubergine relish

In Ballia, where my father's ancestral village is, kichri with aubergine relish (or chokha as the relish is called) is a permanent fixture for lunch every Saturday. It can't be anything else. Sometimes, they serve a rich, spicy mutton curry with it, but otherwise it's just this. Comforting and restorative, it's particularly good on a rainy day. This is in memory of my father, who loved it.

Serves 4

For the burnt aubergine relish
4 large aubergines
12 garlic cloves, peeled
60ml mustard oil
1 red onion, finely chopped
2 green chillies, deseeded and finely chopped
1 teaspoon sea salt
2 tablespoons chopped coriander

For the kichri
120g basmati rice
240g red lentils (or a mixture of red, toor and yellow moong lentils)
1 teaspoon turmeric
4 teaspoons salt
4 tablespoons vegetable oil or ghee
1½ teaspoons cumin seeds
1 dried red chilli
4 garlic cloves, finely chopped
1 onion, finely chopped
100g cauliflower, cut into 1cm florets
1 carrot, diced into 1cm cubes
200g tinned chopped tomatoes
100g petit pois or frozen garden peas
4 tablespoons ghee (optional)

First make the aubergine relish. Using the tip of a sharp knife, cut gashes in the aubergine skin and stuff 3 cloves of garlic into each aubergine. Smear with a little mustard oil, then burn the aubergines over an open flame on the hob for 20–30 minutes, turning frequently to char each one evenly on all sides. (If you have an electric hob, place the aubergines in a roasting tin, drizzle with a little olive oil and roast in the oven at 200°C/180°C fan/Gas mark 6 for 30 minutes.) Once cooked, the aubergines should be soft, with the flesh yielding easily to the touch. When the aubergines are cool enough to handle, remove and discard the skins. Chop the flesh and combine it with the onion, chillies, salt and coriander, and the remaining mustard oil. Mix well and set aside.

Prepare the kichri. Wash the rice and lentils in several changes of water, then leave to soak for 10–15 minutes. Drain and transfer to a large pan, with 2 litres of water. Add the turmeric, bring to the boil, then remove any scum from the surface and add 2 teaspoons of salt. Cook for 25 minutes, until the lentils are completely cooked and collapsed, adding more boiling water from time to time, if the pan looks dry. (The rice will be thoroughly cooked by the time the lentils are done.)

Meanwhile, in a large wok, heat the oil, add the cumin seeds and dried chilli and fry for 1 minute, until the chilli changes colour and the cumin seeds darken and crisp up. Add the chopped garlic, let it colour until golden, then add the onion. Cook for 10–12 minutes, until the onion is lightly golden, then add the cauliflower, carrots and remaining 2 teaspoons of salt. Cook for 6–8 minutes, then add the tomatoes and cook for a further 6–8 minutes, until the sauce has thickened.

Add the cooked rice and lentils to the vegetable pan and mix well. Add more boiling water if it seems too thick, then add the peas and simmer for a couple of minutes, until the rice and lentils are heated through. Remove from the heat and divide the kichri among 4 serving bowls. In a frying pan, heat the ghee to smoking point and pour it over the kichri to scald the top (you can skip this bit if you like). Serve immediately with the relish.

MRS K'S CHICKPEA CURRY

If you search the very back of your kitchen cupboard you're almost guaranteed to come across a long-forgotten bag of dried chickpeas. Rather than blitz them into hummus, why not try your hand at Mrs K's chickpea curry. Nourishing and healthy, this dish saw us through many lockdown nights.

Serves 6

400g dried chickpeas
1 bay leaf
4–5 black peppercorns
1 black cardamom pod
salt

For the curry
1½ tablespoons ground coriander
1 teaspoon mango powder
2 teaspoons powdered pomegranate seeds
2 teaspoons Kasoori methi, crushed to a
    rough powder
1 tablespoon chana masala
1 teaspoon chilli powder
1 tablespoon sunflower oil
1 bay leaf
2 black cardamom pods
2.5cm cinnamon stick
2 whole cloves
10 black peppercorns
1 teaspoon cumin seeds
1 green chilli, slit open, plus extra, chopped,
    to garnish
2cm fresh ginger root, peeled and chopped
chopped coriander leaves, to garnish
naan, kulcha or bhatura, warmed, to serve

Wash the chickpeas and leave them to soak for at least 4 hours or ideally overnight.

Drain the chickpeas then place them in a pan with the bay leaf and whole spices. Season with salt, then cover with water (about 2.5 litres) and place over a medium heat. Bring to the boil, then reduce the heat to a simmer and cook for about 1 hour, until softened.

Drain the chickpeas over a large jug to catch the cooking liquid and discard the bay leaf and whole spices. Set aside.

Make the curry. Mix together the coriander, mango powder, pomegranate, Kasoori methi, chana masala and chilli powder in a bowl and add 125ml of water to make a paste. Set aside.

Heat the sunflower oil in a large, deep-sided frying pan over a medium heat. When hot add the bay leaf, cardamom, cinnamon stick, cloves, peppercorns and cumin seeds and sauté for a few minutes, until they crackle.

Add the spice paste to the whole spices in the pan and cook for 5–7 minutes, until the masala is cooked and starts to catch on the bottom of the pan.

Add the slit green chilli and chopped ginger and sauté for 3–4 minutes. Add 500–750ml of the chickpea cooking liquid and bring to the boil. Stir in the cooked chickpeas, reduce the heat and simmer for around 20–25 minutes, until the liquid is quite thick.

Crush 10–15 per cent of the chickpeas with the back of a spoon to make the gravy thicker, then garnish with chopped coriander and green chilli. Serve with naan, kulcha or bhatura.

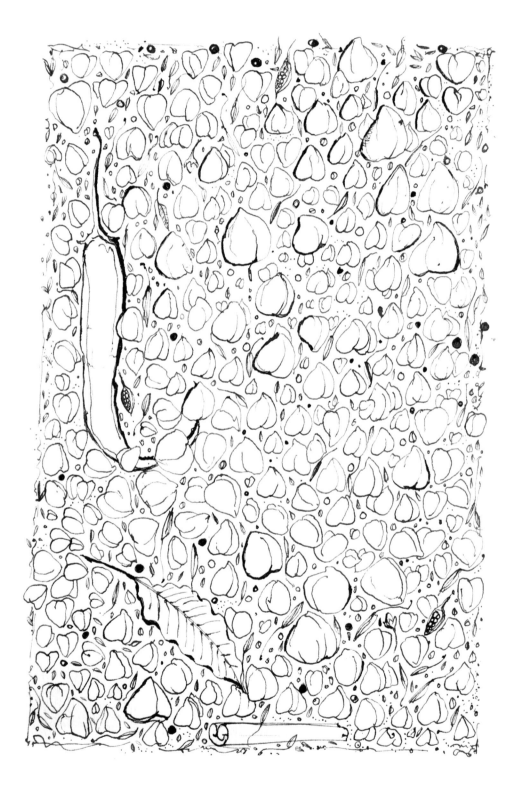

Farokh Talati

BUTTERNUT SQUASH & COCONUT CURRY

Parsis are not known for their love of vegetables, so I wanted to create a dish that had all the signature ingredients and flavours of Parsi cooking and also celebrated a much-loved and widely available vegetable, the humble butternut squash. It is sweet, delicious and holds its own alongside the fiery spices and the flavours of coconut.

Serves 4

2 tablespoons vegetable oil
40g creamed coconut
1 tablespoon ground cumin
1 tablespoon ground coriander
30g desiccated coconut
10 curry leaves
1 x 400g tin of full-fat coconut milk
1 large ripe tomato, diced small
1 tablespoon hot chilli powder
1 teaspoon ground turmeric
2 teaspoons salt
500g squash or pumpkin, peeled, deseeded
    and cut into 2–3cm dice
1 tablespoon apple cider vinegar
1 tablespoon jaggery (use a cheese grater
    to shave off the amount you need)
1 large pinch of saffron
cooked rice or warmed roti, to serve

Heat the oil and creamed coconut on a low heat in a wok, crushing the coconut cream with the back of a spoon. Once the fats have melted, add the cumin and coriander powder and the desiccated coconut and gently fry for 5 minutes, still on a low heat, allowing the coconut to gently brown and become intensely fragrant. Add the curry leaves and allow them to pop and sizzle in the heat for 30 seconds.

Add the coconut milk, then fill the empty tin halfway up with water and add that to the pot too (about 200ml of water). Add the tomato, chilli powder, turmeric, salt and pumpkin or squash. Bring the liquid to the boil, then reduce the heat and simmer for 45 minutes, until the pumpkin or squash is soft through (use the tip of a small knife to give it a poke).

Add the vinegar, jaggery and saffron and stir everything through until the jaggery has dissolved into the sauce. Serve with cooked rice or warmed roti.

Chef's notes...

Jaggery has a unique taste to it that's hard to replicate with anything else, but if necessary you could use 1 teaspoon of caster sugar instead, which will bring out the sweetness.

RATATOUILLE

I now live in France and like to visit my local food market weekly, and during lockdown it has become an important part of my routine. This dish was one I became obsessed with as I learnt to cook. It captures the essence of seasonal Provençale flavours and can be paired with all sorts of things but is just as delicious on its own as a light lunch with a glass of chilled rosé. It pays to take your time when cooking the fondue, allowing the flavours to develop very slowly, and each time you make it you will open up a new universe of discovery ensuring a slightly different result. The aim is to allow each of the individual ingredients to shine, creating an end result so much greater than the sum of its parts.

Cooking and eating should always be a journey of curiosity and excitement, and here the coriander seeds add a wonderful burst of flavour and provide a delicious unexpected freshness as they pop in your mouth.

Serves 4

For the tomato fondue
650g tomatoes
125ml extra-virgin olive oil
1 onion, finely chopped
½ star anise
2 whole cloves
1 teaspoon coriander seeds
2 garlic cloves, crushed or grated
1 bouquet garni (a tied together bunch of thyme, celery leaf, flat-leaf parsley and bay leaf)
several drops of Tabasco sauce
several drops of Worcestershire sauce
1 tablespoon tomato ketchup
250g sherry vinegar
finely grated zest of 1 unwaxed lemon, to taste
10 saffron strands (optional)

For the tomato fondue, skin and deseed the tomatoes, then chop the flesh. Strain and reserve any juice.

Heat the oil in a large pan over a low heat and add the onion, star anise, cloves and coriander seeds. Cook for 10 minutes, then add the garlic and bouquet garni and continue to cook for 15 minutes. Add the chopped tomatoes, strained tomato juices, Tabasco sauce, Worcestershire sauce, ketchup, vinegar and lemon zest. Cook on a low heat for 3–4 hours, adding the saffron (if using) after the first 45 minutes. After 3–4 hours, the mixture will be dark red. You may notice the oil has split from the fondue; do not discard it: pour it off and reserve it for use later.

Make the ratatouille. Keep the aubergines and courgettes separate as you trim them – you're going to cook them at different times. Trim the aubergines and courgettes by removing their skins and about 3mm of flesh. Halve lengthways and remove the very centres of each (where the seeds are) and reserve for another use.

Very finely dice the aubergines into 3mm pieces. Do the same with the courgettes. Place the aubergines into a sieve set over a bowl and sprinkle 2–3 teaspoons of salt over them. Leave for 10 minutes, then thoroughly rinse them under cold, running water.

While the aubergines are 'bleeding', trim the fennel, discarding the outer layer. Dice as finely as the aubergines and courgettes. Set aside.

Chargrill the red peppers. Heat the grill to hot. Halve the peppers and remove the pith and seeds. Rub the halves with a little olive oil and arrange them, skin side up, on a grill pan. Put them under the grill and leave until they completely blacken (about 10–12 minutes). Transfer the peppers to a heatproof bowl and cover the bowl tightly with cling film. Leave for 5 minutes, then remove the cling film and peel away the skins. Run the peeled peppers under cold, running water, then dice the flesh into small pieces.

Place a fine-meshed sieve over a bowl.

For the ratatouille
3 aubergines
3 courgettes
1 fennel bulb
2 red peppers
extra-virgin olive oil
2–3 teaspoons thyme leaves
10 pitted black olives, finely chopped
10 basil leaves
10 coriander seeds
salt and freshly ground black pepper

Add enough olive oil to a pan to cover the base by about 1–2mm. (Choose a pan large enough to hold the diced aubergine in a single layer.) Place over a medium–high heat and when the oil is hot, but not smoking, add the aubergines, cooking for 4 minutes before tipping them into the sieve to drain off the oil into the bowl. Once the aubergines are drained, tip them into a separate bowl. Season them with salt and freshly ground black pepper and stir in a ½ teaspoon of the picked thyme leaves.

Using a fresh batch of olive oil, repeat the process with the courgettes, cooking for only 2 minutes on a slightly lower heat. Drain the courgettes in the sieve (reserving the oil), then transfer them to a bowl and season with salt and pepper. Again, stir in a ½ teaspoon of the thyme leaves.

Finally, cook the fennel in another batch of oil – this time on a moderately low heat for 6–8 minutes. Drain as before, reserving the oil.

Combine all the cooked vegetables with the chopped olives and 250g of the tomato fondue. Finely slice the basil and add it along with the remaining thyme leaves and the coriander seeds. Finally, mix together the reserved oil from the top of the tomato fondue with all the reserved oil from frying the vegetables and mix them into the ratatouille, to taste. Season as needed before serving.

You can make the ratatouille up to 1 day ahead of serving and reheat in a moderate oven for 5 minutes.

Chantelle Nicholson

AUTUMN VEGETABLE SAVOURY BREAD PUDDING

This is a great dish to use up any day-old or stale bread. It is pretty simple to put together, then just needs baking when you are almost ready to eat. Feel free to use up any leftover cooked vegetables, grains or pulses – the more the merrier! I like this served with a peppery green salad or with wilted spinach or chard on the side.

Serves 4

25g unsalted butter
4 slices of day-old or stale bread
2 eggs
175ml whole milk
2 tablespoons olive oil
1 onion, halved and sliced
4 tablespoons tomato purée
200g tinned chopped tomatoes
2 tablespoons balsamic vinegar
200g white or red cabbage, finely sliced
200g kale, roughly chopped
100g lentils, barley, split peas or brown rice,
    cooked according to packet instructions
200g baked butternut or kuri squash, chopped
200g cheddar, grated
salt and freshly ground black pepper

Preheat the oven to 180°C/160°C fan/Gas mark 4.

Using the butter, grease a 20–28cm casserole dish. Arrange half of the bread slices on the bottom, overlapping if needs be. Blend or whisk the eggs and milk together, seasoning well with salt and pepper. Pour half of this over the bread and allow to sit while you make the filling.

Heat the olive oil in a frying pan and, when hot, add the onion. Season well with salt and cook for about 5–7 minutes over a medium heat, until golden. Add the tomato purée and mix well, then add the chopped tomatoes and balsamic vinegar. Cook for 2 minutes, then add in the cabbage and kale and cook for 5 minutes. Add the legumes or grains and the squash. Cook for 2 minutes, then remove from the heat.

Add half the tomato mixture to the casserole dish, on top of the soaked bread. Add half the grated cheese and a good grinding of pepper. Arrange the remaining bread slices on top and pour over the remaining egg and milk mixture. Top with the remaining tomato mixture, then scatter over the rest of the grated cheese.

Cover and place in the oven for 20 minutes, then remove the cover and bake for a further 10 minutes, until golden. Serve hot.

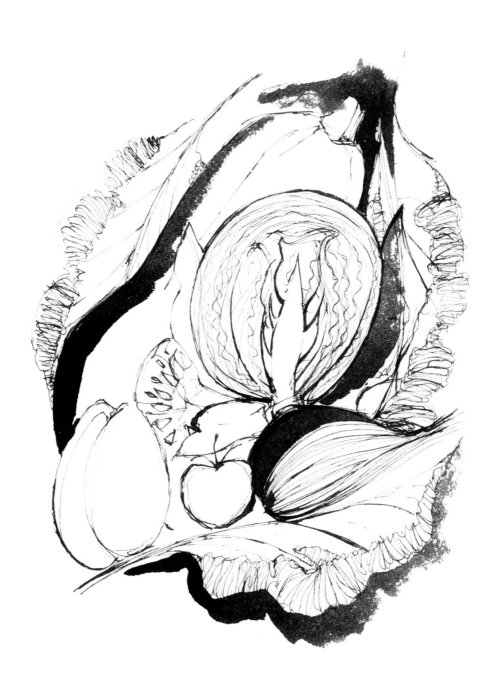

Robin Gill

PASTA NERANO

Pasta Nerano originates from an amazing restaurant called Maria Grazia, which sits on a stunning rocky beach called Marina Del Cantone on the gulf of Napoli. I worked near there a good few years back and lived in a little apartment in Nerano. That's where Sarah and I fell in love and we try to return there every other year. We got married in Tuscany and we took a gang of our closest pals to Nerano, on the first leg of our honeymoon – that's why, to Sarah, this dish is always 'honeymoon pasta'.

Feel free to use ordinary courgettes if you cannot find Romanesco, and use parmesan if you are unable to find provolone.

Serves 4–6

olive oil, for frying
800g Romanesco courgettes, sliced into
    thin rounds
400g dried spaghetti
2 or 3 garlic cloves, peeled and crushed
200g provolone cheese, grated
a few basil leaves, plus extra to garnish
salt and freshly ground black pepper

Heat a little olive oil in a frying pan and, in batches if necessary, fry the courgette slices in a single layer until they are lightly browned. Set aside each batch to drain on kitchen paper while you fry the next. Then, sprinkle lightly with salt.

Bring a large pan of salted water to the boil. Add the spaghetti and cook until very al dente – about 8 minutes.

While the spaghetti is cooking, heat a little more olive oil in a large sauté or frying pan. Add the garlic and sauté lightly over a medium heat, until lightly golden in colour.

When the pasta is done, drain it, but not too well, and reserve some of the cooking water. Transfer the pasta to the frying pan and add the courgette rounds (reserve some for garnish, if you like) and a ladleful of pasta water. Mix everything together vigorously for a minute or two, then add the grated cheese and some basil leaves, and continue mixing until the cheese has completely melted into a creamy sauce, adding more pasta water if you need to keep things flowing smoothly.

Serve your spaghetti right away, garnished with any remaining courgette slices and a basil leaf or two.

GNOCCHI
with mushroom ragù

*This traditional homemade Italian pasta is well
worth making from scratch. These little golden
potato pasta nuggets, smothered in classic ragù,
are satisfyingly moreish and perfect for lunch or
dinner to wow friends and family alike.*

Serves 6

450g chestnut mushrooms, sliced
100g unsalted butter
few thyme sprigs
vegetarian Italian hard cheese, grated, to serve

For the ragù
2 tablespoons olive oil
1 onion, finely chopped
1 carrot, finely chopped
1 celery stick, finely chopped
4 garlic cloves, finely chopped
150g tomato purée
250ml red wine
200ml port
450ml strong vegetable stock
1 tablespoon rosemary leaves
1 tablespoon thyme leaves

For the gnocchi
600g floury potatoes (such as Maris Piper),
    peeled and cut into 3–4cm pieces
1 large egg
450g white pasta flour (tipo 00)
salt and freshly ground black pepper

First, prepare the ragù. Heat the oil in a heavy-based
pan over a medium–high heat. When hot, add the onion,
carrot, celery and garlic and fry for 5 minutes, until soft.
Add the tomato purée, stir, and cook for 7–8 minutes,
until the mixture is a rich red. This really releases so
much tomatoey flavour, so take your time!

Add the wine, port, stock, rosemary and thyme, bring
the sauce to the boil and simmer for 1 hour, stirring
occasionally, until thickened.

While the sauce is simmering, prepare the gnocchi.
Boil the spuds for about 25 minutes, until soft. Drain
them, but don't add any water to cool them – leave
them to cool in the colander. When the potatoes are
cool enough to handle, pass them through a ricer into
a bowl, or tip them into a bowl and mash until
completely smooth.

Make a well in the centre of the potatoes, add the egg
and season with salt and pepper. Add the flour and mix
to form a dough, then knead it for a few minutes.

Divide the gnocchi into 4 or 5 equal pieces. Using
your hands, roll out each piece into a 2cm-diameter
rope, then cut along the length of each rope at
2.5mm intervals.

Bring a pan of salted water to the boil. Add the gnocchi,
and as they rise to the surface (this will take 3–4 minutes
or so), scoop them out using a slotted spoon and add
them to the ragù.

Just before serving, fry the mushrooms in the butter
with the thyme sprigs for 5 minutes, until softened.

To serve, divide the gnocchi and ragù between
6 bowls, top with equal amounts of the mushrooms
and generously sprinkle with the grated cheese.

James Cochran

CELERIAC TAGLIATELLE
with seaweed, Cornish cured mackerel & 'nduja

This is definitely a meal to impress, and it was one I made when I wanted a little luxury during lockdown – just because we weren't able to do the things we love or see family and friends in person didn't mean we couldn't treat ourselves and make a meal of it every once in a while.

You can use any leftover seaweed butter to fry up some sole or grill with scallops.

Serves 10

200g 'nduja
1 celeriac (about 1kg), peeled

For the seaweed butter
sunflower oil
¼ onion, chopped
½ teaspoon salt
½ tablespoon nori powder
15g parmesan, grated
125g unsalted butter, at room temperature

For the cured mackerel
300ml mirin
100ml dark soy sauce
50ml fish sauce
2 garlic cloves, crushed
zest of 1 orange
10 mackerel fillets, each one about 125–150g

First, prepare the 'nduja. Preheat the oven to 85°C/65°C fan/Gas ¼–½ and break up the 'nduja. Place it on a baking tray lined with a clean j-cloth and cook for 10 hours until it resembles crumbs. Drain well. Hand chop.

Using a spiraliser, spiral the celeriac (if you don't have a spiraliser, very, very thinly slice it). Bring a pan of water to a simmer and blanch the celeriac for 1 minute, then refresh it in iced water. Drain it and weigh it into six 75g portions. Set aside until needed.

Make the seaweed butter. Heat a little sunflower oil in a frying pan over a low heat until hot. Add the onion and sweat for 20 minutes, until soft. Add the salt, nori and parmesan, stir to combine, then remove from the heat and set aside to cool.

Put the butter in a stand mixer fitted with the beater and whip it until it is pale and fluffy. Fold in the cooled onion and nori mixture and place it all in the fridge to chill.

For the mackerel, combine all the ingredients except the mackerel itself in a bowl, to make a marinade. Score the mackerel fillets, making cuts along the length of each, about 1cm apart, and add them to the bowl with the marinade. Leave to marinate for 20 minutes.

When you're ready to serve, drain the mackerel well, discarding the marinade. Using a kitchen blow torch, scorch the skin side of the fillets for about 40 seconds, until blackened.

Weigh the seaweed butter and add an equal weight of water to a pan. Place over a medium heat and, once simmering, add the butter, a little at a time, until you have a creamy sauce. Add the celeriac and heat through for 2 minutes to soften the veg. Check the seasoning and divide the celeriac equally over 10 serving plates. Top equally with the mackerel fillets and scatter with the 'nduja, then serve immediately.

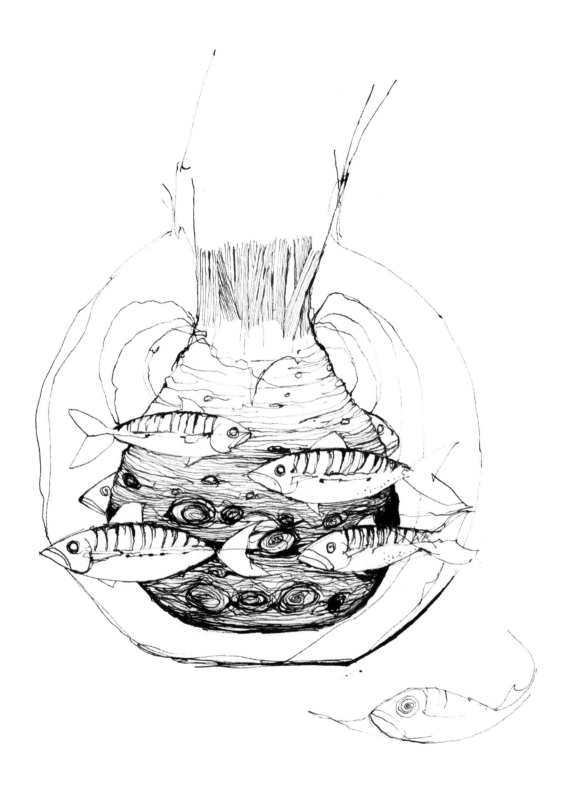

RIGATONI
with cavolo nero, pecorino & pangrattato

I love this robust, winter pasta, especially as it uses so few ingredients. It's completely vegetarian but has as much flavour and power as a meat ragù, largely because of the salty pecorino and the intensity of the black cabbage (cavolo nero).

This recipe is typically Sicilian in the way that nothing goes to waste. The pasta is cooked in the cabbage water for maximum flavour and it's finished with my favourite fried breadcrumbs (made from day-old bread, of course). It's a frugal composition, but much more than a sum of its parts.

Serves 4

extra-virgin olive oil
1 large or 2 small slices of day-old sourdough
    bread, roughly chopped into a coarse crumb
500–700g cavolo nero (according to
    taste), woody stalks discarded, leaves
    roughly chopped
500g rigatoni pasta
100g pecorino, finely grated
sea salt

Add a good splash of olive oil to a frying pan. Set over a medium heat and fry the breadcrumbs until crisp and golden brown. Season with sea salt, then drain and reserve.

Place a medium pan of salted water over a high heat and bring to the boil. Plunge in the cabbage and cook for 5 minutes or so, on a rolling boil, until tender. Immediately use tongs or a slotted spoon to transfer the cabbage to a blender, along with a ladleful of the cooking water. Blend to a smooth, thick, deep-green purée, transfer to a large frying pan and reserve.

Now cook the pasta in the remaining cabbage water until al dente, then transfer the pasta to the cabbage purée with a good lug of olive oil and half the pecorino. Reserve the cooking water.

Turn on the heat, add a ladleful of the cooking water and toss the pasta through the cabbage purée to coat. Divide the pasta equally between 4 bowls and top with the remaining pecorino and the fried breadcrumbs.

Mark Hix

CUTTLEFISH INK SPELT

This isn't a risotto in the true sense of the word, but more a sort of British version of Spanish arroz negro. You can use cuttlefish or squid for this dish and you will need to order the little sachets of ink from your fishmonger in advance. If you can't get hold of squid ink, then make a white version and finish with a handful of chopped soft herbs.

Serves 4

2 tablespoons rapeseed oil
200g spelt, soaked in cold water for 3–4 hours, then drained
50g (6 sachets) squid ink
1 litre fish stock
120g unsalted butter
150g cleaned squid, cut into small, rough 2–3cm squares
1 tablespoon chopped hedgerow or three-cornered garlic or garlic chives
1 tablespoon chopped flat-leaf parsley
1 tablespoon chopped chervil

Heat the rapeseed oil in a heavy-bottomed saucepan. Add the drained spelt and stir on a low heat for a minute or so without allowing the spelt to colour.

Add the squid ink, stir well, then gradually add the stock, a ladle or two at a time, stirring continuously and ensuring that all the liquid has been absorbed before adding more.

When you have added most of the stock and the spelt is tender and cooked, stir in two-thirds of the butter and a little more of the remaining stock if the risotto seems a bit too dry – the consistency should be wet but not runny.

Meanwhile, place a heavy frying pan on a medium heat. When hot, add the rest of the butter and allow to melt. Increase the heat to high, add the squid and cook for 1 minute or so, until cooked through, then stir in the herbs.

To serve, spoon the spelt on to warmed serving plates and scatter the squid over.

SEA BASS
with braised shallots, spinach & beurre blanc

This classic dish is one of life's pleasures – it works perfectly with sea bass, but you can make it with any white fish, such as cod or bream. Braised shallots are a great accompaniment not just to this dish, but to a roast dinner too. This is simplicity at its very best.

Serves 4

8 banana shallots, halved
1 teaspoon caster sugar
50ml olive oil
1 thyme sprig
50g unsalted butter
200ml chicken stock
8 farmed sea bass fillets (each about 60g)
400g spinach
salt

For the beurre blanc
4 banana shallots, finely chopped
50ml dry white wine
50ml white wine vinegar
200g unsalted butter, cubed and chilled
50ml double cream
1 teaspoon salt

Season the shallots with salt and turn them in the sugar. Put 1 tablespoon of the oil into a saucepan, add the thyme, then add the shallots cut side down. Cook for 2–3 minutes, adding half the butter halfway through, until the shallots are nicely browned, then add the chicken stock. Cover and very gently simmer for 15–20 minutes, until the shallots are braised and tender. Add a splash of water if the pan gets too dry at any point. Set aside and keep warm.

Heat the grill to hot.

Make the beurre blanc. Place the shallots in a saucepan and add the wine, vinegar and 50ml of water. Cook over a medium heat, allowing the liquid to reduce until it completely evaporates, leaving only the shallots. Slowly whisk in half the cubes of cold butter. Add the cream and continue whisking, while adding the remaining butter. Bring the sauce to a simmer and allow it to bubble and thicken. Season with the salt. Keep warm.

Season the sea bass fillets well and place them on a baking tray, skin side up, under a hot grill for 4–5 minutes without turning, until just cooked through.

Meanwhile, sauté the spinach in the remaining oil and butter until wilted. Season with sea salt.

To serve, divide the spinach equally between 4 plates and top each portion with 2 fillets of sea bass. Add the braised shallots, and drizzle over some of the beurre blanc. Keep the remainder in a jug on the side for people to help themselves.

SMOKED SALMON & SPINACH LASAGNE

This comforting pasta bake is easy to prepare and always popular. The recipe is based on a Scandinavian dish that my wife Michaela has been making for years. It's absolutely delicious and has the added advantage that it can be prepared in advance, ready to bake and serve when required.

Serves 4

100g unsalted butter, plus extra for greasing
100g plain flour
950ml whole milk
1 tablespoon Dijon mustard
½ teaspoon grated nutmeg
½ leek, cut into thin strips
400g baby spinach
2 garlic cloves, crushed
8–10 lasagne sheets
500g smoked salmon, cut into 2cm squares
250g cheddar, grated
50g parmesan, grated
4 dill sprigs, chopped
salt and freshly ground black pepper
green salad, to serve

Melt 75g of the butter in a heavy-based saucepan over a medium heat. Add the flour and cook out for 1–2 minutes, then slowly add the milk, stirring as you go. Cook for 8–10 minutes, stirring continuously without letting the sauce boil too hard, until thickened. Once thickened, add the mustard and nutmeg.

Preheat the oven to 180°C/160°C fan/Gas mark 4 and grease a lasagne dish with butter.

Melt the remaining 25g of butter in a saucepan, add the leek and cook for 2–3 minutes to soften a little. Season with salt and pepper, then add the spinach leaves (a handful at a time is easier) and the garlic and cook for a further 2–3 minutes, until the spinach has wilted. Drain off the excess liquid.

Spread some of the sauce over the bottom of the dish and place a layer of lasagne sheets on top. Top with some of the leek and spinach mixture, then some smoked salmon. Sprinkle over some cheddar and parmesan. Repeat the process, finishing the top layer with sauce, a few pieces of salmon, and grated cheese. Bake for 45 minutes, until golden and the lasagne is tender. (To check if the lasagne is cooked, insert a fork – if there's no resistance, it's ready.)

Sprinkle the dill over the top and serve with a fresh green salad.

FISH & CHIPS
with mushy peas

This is a great recipe for a traditional family favourite. I've used gurnard as it's a flavoursome and sustainable alternative to the usual cod or haddock, but other white fish, such as hake, will work equally well. Don't worry too much about the herbs, you can change them to use whatever is available at the time. Using gluten-free flour makes the batter lighter and means that those who are gluten intolerant can enjoy the dish too!

Serves 4

1 teaspoon chopped tarragon leaves
1 teaspoon chopped chives
1 teaspoon chopped flat-leaf parsley
4 gurnard fillets, each weighing 130g

For the tartare sauce
3 egg yolks
1 tablespoon white wine vinegar
1 teaspoon English mustard
250ml rapeseed oil
2 gherkins, finely diced
2 teaspoons capers, drained and chopped
1 heaped tablespoon jalapeños in brine from
   a jar, drained and chopped
2 hard-boiled eggs, chopped
sea salt and freshly ground black pepper

For the batter
200g gluten-free self-raising flour
200ml dry sparkling cider

For the mushy peas
150g frozen peas
150g tinned mushy peas
50g salted butter
2 tablespoons finely chopped mint leaves
2 tablespoons finely chopped marjoram leaves
½ teaspoon malt vinegar

For the chips
6 large Maris Piper potatoes
vegetable oil, for frying

First, make the tartare sauce. Whisk the egg yolks, vinegar and mustard together in a large bowl until well combined. Slowly add the rapeseed oil in a steady stream, continuing to whisk until you have a thick mayonnaise.

Add the gherkins to the mayonnaise along with the capers and jalapeños. Finally, fold in the hard-boiled eggs. Taste and adjust the seasoning with salt and pepper, as necessary. Store in the fridge until ready to serve.

For the batter, put the flour into a large bowl, then whisk in the cider to combine thoroughly, so that the mixture is smooth and lump-free. Move to a cool place until you're ready to fry.

For the mushy peas, bring the peas to the boil in a saucepan of lightly salted water. Drain, then place in a large bowl with the mushy peas, butter and herbs. Using a hand blender, blitz to the desired consistency. Return to the pan and add the malt vinegar. Heat through gently, but don't allow the mixture to boil. Keep warm until you're ready to serve.

For the chips, peel the potatoes and cut them into nice chunky chips. Put the chips into a saucepan, cover with cold water and add a good pinch of salt. Bring to the boil and cook for about 5 minutes, until still slightly raw in the centre, then drain well and cool.

Pour in enough vegetable oil to half fill a deep-fat fryer or large, heavy-based saucepan and heat to 180°C. Once the oil has come up to temperature, put the chips into the fryer basket, then plunge the basket into the hot oil. Cook the chips until golden brown, remove from the fryer and allow all the oil to drip off. Turn out on to a tray lined with kitchen paper to dry. Season generously with sea salt and keep warm. Keep the oil hot.

To cook the fish, quickly give the batter a stir to ensure it is smooth. Put the chopped herbs on to

a plate and place the fish on top. Press down gently so that the herbs stick to the fish. Turn the fish fillets over and press again to collect all the herbs. Pass each fillet of fish through the batter to evenly coat, then carefully drop each one into the fryer or pan of hot oil. Cook for 6–8 minutes, until golden brown. (Note: always drop items into the fryer away from your body so the oil does not splash back!)

Carefully remove the fish once cooked and drain on kitchen paper.

To serve, place the fish on top of the chips and serve with the mushy peas and a good dollop of tartare sauce.

Paul Ainsworth

CORNISH COD PIPERADE
with Cornish mussels & basil mayonnaise

This cod piperade was born out of lockdown. I would visit our businesses most days and see the fishermen selling their amazing seafood at the end of the quay in Padstow – lobsters, crabs, turbot, John Dory and much more. With restaurants closed, these fishermen lost their income overnight so I wanted to do anything I could to help support them. As a start, I bought some cod and this recipe was created from ingredients that we had in the cupboard and some veg in the fridge that needed using up. It became this lovely Spanish-inspired stew that is a now a staple in the Ainsworth household.

Serves 4

1 whole cod fillet (about 400g), or other
   white fish
1kg mussels
250ml white wine
1–2 tablespoons olive oil
250g good-quality chorizo, cut into
   thick rounds
1 onion, thinly sliced
1 green pepper, deseeded and cut into strips
1 yellow pepper, deseeded and cut into strips
1 red pepper, deseeded and cut into strips
1 small red or green chilli, deseeded and
   thinly sliced
4 garlic cloves, thinly sliced
1 teaspoon smoked paprika
1 punnet vine-ripened baby plum tomatoes,
   halved, vine reserved
200g good-quality passata
1 x 400g tin of chickpeas
75g basil leaves, roughly chopped
sea salt and cracked black pepper

For the basil mayonnaise
75g good-quality mayonnaise
3 teaspoons pesto
finely grated parmesan, to taste
finely grated unwaxed lemon zest, to taste

Lightly salt the cod fillet with sea salt and leave for 1 hour. Gently wash off the excess salt, pat dry and portion the fillet into 4 steaks.

Place a casserole pan on a medium–high heat. Once hot, add the mussels and white wine. Place the lid on the pan and steam the mussels for 1–2 minutes, until they begin to open their shells (discard any that stay shut). Using a slotted spoon, remove the mussels from the juice and pour the juice into a jug to use later.

Place the casserole pan back on a medium heat and add a little olive oil. Add the chorizo and allow to sauté for 2–3 minutes, until crisp. Using a slotted spoon, remove the chorizo from the pan, leaving the lovely oil behind. Add the onion, lower the heat, and roast it in the beautiful orange oil for about 5–7 minutes, until softened. Next add the peppers, chilli, garlic and smoked paprika. Continue to roast off all the ingredients for about 5 minutes over a low–medium heat. Add the tomatoes and let them caramelise away for about 3–5 minutes, until they start to go mushy.

Preheat the oven to 180°C/160°C fan/Gas mark 4.

Add the passata, chickpeas, mussel cooking juice, vines and chorizo to the pan, and bring the liquid to a simmer. Cook for about 10 minutes, or until the stew is nice and thick. Stir in your mussels and place your pieces of cod on top of the stew, put a lid on the pan and place in the oven. Cook for 5 minutes, then check the doneness of the fillets – depending on thickness, they could take 8–10 minutes, or even a little longer, until translucent and perfectly cooked. (The best way to check if the fish is cooked is with a temperature probe – insert the probe at the thickest part of the fillet and when it reaches 44°C, your fish will be lovely and translucent every time.)

While the stew is cooking, prepare the basil mayonnaise by simply mixing all the ingredients together in a bowl.

Take the stew out of the oven and season with cracked pepper. Sprinkle over the chopped basil and serve with a dollop of the basil mayonnaise.

Richard Corrigan

BENTLEY'S FISH PIE

For me this recipe is a taste of home, reminding me of time spent in Ireland by the sea. It's my go-to for when I'm tired or stressed, or just need a bit of comfort. It's a really versatile recipe and can be made with different kinds of fish, just try and get a smoked fish in there for its distinct flavour.

Serves 4

1kg mixed skin-on boneless fish fillets, including salmon, prawns, smoked haddock and white fish
7–8 floury potatoes (1kg), peeled and cut into equal-sized pieces
2 egg yolks
a little lemon juice
handful of fresh breadcrumbs
a little grated parmesan
garden peas and spinach, steamed until tender, to serve

For the sauce
100g unsalted butter, plus a little extra for sweating the vegetables
1 onion, chopped
2 garlic cloves, crushed
1 thyme sprig, leaves picked
150ml white wine
smoked haddock trimmings (see above)
1 litre whole milk
100g plain flour
1 tablespoon English mustard, plus extra if needed
handful of flat-leaf parsley, chopped
salt and freshly ground black pepper

Remove the skin from the fish (reserve the smoked haddock skin for the sauce) and cut the flesh into bite-sized pieces. Set aside while you start the sauce.

Heat a little butter in a saucepan over a medium heat. When melted and hot, add the onion, garlic and thyme and sweat for about 10–15 minutes, until softened. Add the white wine and the smoked haddock trimmings and cook for a few minutes to burn off the alcohol. Add the milk and bring to just under the boil, then take the pan from the heat, pass the contents through a sieve into a heatproof bowl and keep hot.

Melt the 100g of butter in a heavy-based saucepan, add the flour and cook over a low heat, stirring for 5 minutes. Pour the hot, infused milk into the pan and vigorously whisk until the mixture is smooth and thick. Taste to make sure you can't taste the flour. If you can, let it cook gently for a little longer.

Whisk in the mustard and add the parsley. Check the seasoning and season with salt and pepper and more mustard, if you wish. Leave to cool down while you make the mash — it is best not to assemble the pie with hot sauce as it will cook the fish too quickly.

Preheat the oven to 180°C/160°C fan/Gas mark 4.

Cook the potatoes in boiling salted water until tender (how long this takes will depend on how large you chopped them). Drain them in a colander and allow to steam for a couple of minutes. Then mash them and season. Beat in the egg yolks. Scoop the hot mash into a piping bag, if you have one (it needs to be hot in order to pipe easily), otherwise you can use a spoon.

To assemble, spoon a little of the sauce into the bottom of a pie dish. Arrange the selection of fish on top of the sauce. Season with salt and pepper and a little lemon juice. Completely cover with sauce, then pipe or spoon on the mash. Mix together the breadcrumbs and parmesan and sprinkle the crust mixture over the top. Place the pie on a baking sheet and cook for about 20 minutes, until the fish is cooked through and the top is golden brown. Serve immediately with garden peas and spinach.

SALMON EN PAPILLOTE

This is a really easy but impressive recipe to serve at the table. I've suggested quantities for the marinade, but it's really flexible, so feel free to amend depending on your personal preference. The salad is super-fresh and the perfect accompaniment to the fish.

Serves 6

1kg salmon fillet, skin removed and pin boned

For the marinade
50g fresh ginger root, peeled and grated
4 garlic cloves, grated or crushed
100ml miso paste
splash of light soy sauce
1 red chilli, deseeded and sliced
dash of mirin
dash of fish sauce
pinch of salt

For the salad
300g egg noodles, cooked
1 red chilli, deseeded and chopped
1 red pepper, deseeded and sliced into strips
½ red onion, sliced
1½ tablespoons chopped pickled ginger
1 small courgette, finely sliced
2 tablespoons peanuts, toasted and
   roughly chopped
1 handful of mint, leaves picked and torn
1 handful of coriander, leaves picked
   and chopped
1 handful of basil, leaves picked and torn
2 tablespoons cashews, toasted and
   roughly chopped
2 handfuls of beansprouts
1 small carrot, peeled and cut into matchsticks

Combine all the marinade ingredients in a bowl and set aside.

Place the salmon on a piece of baking paper cut large enough to fully enclose the fish. Set the salmon on the paper into a baking tray. Cover with the marinade, then wrap the fish in the baking paper like a parcel, and marinate in the fridge for 1–2 hours.

Preheat the oven to 180°C/160°C fan/Gas mark 4. Once marinated, cook the salmon parcel for 12–15 minutes, until the internal temperature of the salmon is showing 40°C on a cooking thermometer (or until the fish is opaque, or cooked through to your liking). Remove the fish from the oven and let it rest for 5 minutes.

Meanwhile, combine the salad ingredients in a bowl.

Open the fish parcel at the table and allow everyone to dig in, with spoonfuls of the salad alongside.

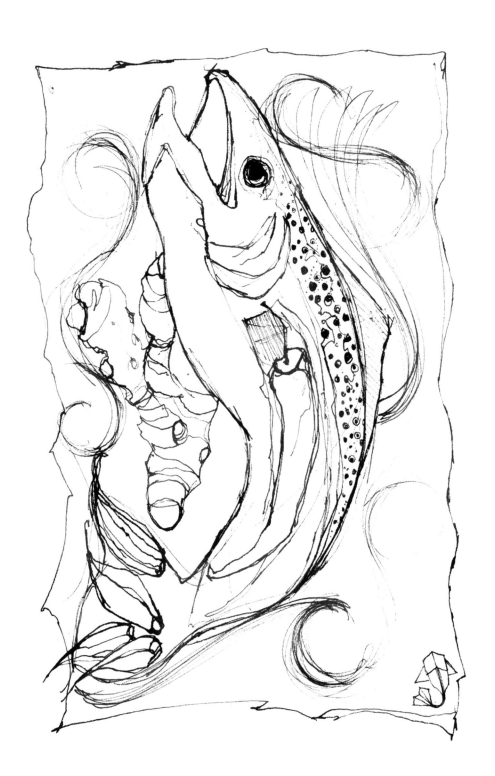

Tom Brown

HAKE KIEVS
with mushroom butter & hollandaise

Kievs are classic comfort food and great to make from scratch. Here's my take on the timeless kiev, using hake rather than the traditional chicken.

If you have too much mushroom butter, it freezes well and works nicely melted and finished with a little lemon juice as a butter sauce.

Serves 4

4 x 120g skinless, boneless hake fillets
   (skinned and pin boned)
100g plain flour
1 egg, beaten
100g panko breadcrumbs

For the mushroom butter
250g unsalted butter, softened at
   room temperature
handful of small wild mushrooms
   (chanterelles, girolles or shimeji are ideal)
30g pine nuts, toasted
35g parmesan, finely grated
1 garlic clove, crushed
1 tablespoon ground dried porcini mushrooms
1 teaspoon table salt

For the hollandaise
3 egg yolks
1 teaspoon Dijon mustard
1 tablespoon white wine vinegar
good pinch of sea salt
300ml light olive oil
3–4 tablespoons truffle oil
juice of ½ lemon

To make the mushroom butter, melt a little of the butter in a frying pan over a medium heat and fry the mushrooms for 3–4 minutes, until soft and with a light golden colour. Set aside to cool.

Blend the remaining butter with the rest of the ingredients in a food processor until smooth and evenly incorporated. Chop the fried mushrooms, then add to the butter and mix through. Set aside until needed.

Slice horizontally along the side of the hake fillets three-quarters of the way through to butterfly them, and open them out. Spoon some of the butter mixture into the centre of the unfolded hake, and fold the fish over to seal in the butter. Wrap each portion tightly in cling film then leave to set in the fridge for at least 1 hour, although overnight is fine, to firm up.

Once firm, unwrap the fish portions. Tip the flour on to a plate, put the egg into a bowl and tip the panko on to another plate, ready to coat the fish. Working with each fish in turn, run it through the flour, then the beaten egg, then the panko, and then back into the egg and panko to 'double breadcrumb' (this will ensure the butter doesn't leak out). Set aside while you make the hollandaise.

Mix the egg yolks, mustard, vinegar and 1 tablespoon of water together in a metal bowl with the sea salt. Set the bowl over a pan of gently simmering water and whisk continuously, until the mixture becomes light, fluffy and full of air. You should be able to trace a figure of eight on the surface and it stay in place. Remove the pan from the heat and gradually drip in the olive and truffle oils together to emulsify and make a glossy sauce, whisking to incorporate as you do so. Whisk in the lemon juice, then set aside at room temperature.

Preheat a deep fryer to 180°C and your oven to 200°C/180°C fan/Gas mark 6. Two at a time, carefully drop the Kievs into the oil for 2–3 minutes per batch, until golden brown and crispy. Remove them from the oil and place on a baking tray while you cook the rest. Then, transfer the tray to the oven and bake the Kievs for 3–4 minutes, until hot throughout and thoroughly cooked. Serve with a large spoonful of the hollandaise and enjoy!

FILLET OF MACKEREL
with shaved fennel salad & soy
lime glaze

*Mackerel is one of the most plentiful species
of fish in our seas; but to appreciate this fish at
its best, it must be very fresh. This little dish has
the virtue of being very simple, but packed
with flavours.*

Serves 4

4 skin-on mackerel fillets

For the fennel salad
150g fennel bulb, trimmed
15g rocket leaves
juice of ¼ lime
4 teaspoons extra-virgin olive oil
pinch of sea salt
pinch of freshly ground white pepper
1 teaspoon fennel seeds, soaked in warm
    water for 2 hours, then drained and toasted
    in a dry pan

For the glaze
2 tablespoons light soy sauce
1 tablespoon light muscovado sugar
1 teaspoon finely chopped fresh ginger root
½ teaspoon lime juice

Prepare the fennel for the salad. Remove the core
from the fennel, then use a mandoline to cut it into
wafer-thin slices. Immerse the fennel in a bowl of iced
water and set it aside for 20 minutes.

Meanwhile, make the glaze. In a small saucepan,
combine 1 tablespoon of water with the soy sauce,
sugar, ginger and lime juice. Place over a low–medium
heat and bring to the boil. Let the glaze bubble for
10 seconds only, then remove it from the heat and
set aside.

Preheat your grill to high. Check the mackerel for
pin bones and lightly score the skin at 2cm intervals.
Place the mackerel fillets, skin-side upwards, on a baking
tray. Place the fish under the hot grill for 4–5 minutes,
depending on the thickness of the fillets, until
just cooked.

While the mackerel is under the grill, drain the fennel,
pat it dry with a tea towel and place in a large bowl with
the rocket leaves, lime juice, extra-virgin olive oil, sea
salt and white pepper. Toss everything lightly together
to combine and sprinkle with the toasted fennel seeds.

To serve, divide the salad between 4 individual plates
and lay the grilled mackerel fillets on top. Spoon the
glaze over and around the fish. Serve immediately.

Clare Smyth

CHARRED CHILLI CHICKEN
with jasmine rice

This is a super-easy, quick and delicious recipe that I have cooked at home for more than 20 years. Since opening Core, it has also become a team favourite as a hearty meal before dinner service. As the days get colder and you are looking for a meal that delivers warmth and comfort, is easy to prepare, with a few, inexpensive ingredients, and can be shared happily among family and friends – this is the one.

Serves 4

For the chicken and rice
8 skinless, boneless chicken thighs, diced
300g jasmine rice
250ml vegetable oil
4 red chillies, halved lengthways
80g fresh ginger root, peeled and finely diced
80ml chicken stock
240ml light soy sauce
180ml rice wine vinegar
4 spring onions, sliced
40g coriander, leaves and stems chopped
120g peanuts, toasted and chopped

For the marinade
350ml light soy sauce
350ml rice wine vinegar
60g cornflour

First, mix the marinade ingredients together in a bowl. Then, add the diced chicken, turn to coat and set aside in the fridge to marinate for 1 hour.

Place the jasmine rice in a saucepan with 600ml of water and cook according to the packet instructions. Once the rice is cooked, drain if necessary and cover to keep warm.

Place a large, deep frying pan or a wok over a medium–high heat and add the oil. When hot, add the chillies and cook until they start to blacken, then using a slotted spoon, remove them from the oil and set aside.

Remove the chicken from the marinade. Add the pieces to the hot oil and fry until golden. Add the ginger, then cook for a couple of minutes, then add the chicken stock, soy sauce and rice wine vinegar. Bring the liquid to the boil and cook for a further couple of minutes, until the chicken is cooked through.

Transfer the chicken to a big bowl. Top with the spring onions, coriander, nuts and finally the charred chillies. Serve with the rice alongside.

CHICKEN SCHNITZEL

This heartening dish became a family favourite during lockdown. Succulent chicken with a crispy outer shell, creamy smooth mash and zingy salsa verde offered comfort in those first uncertain weeks and soon became a family staple. Serve with a wedge of lemon to make even more flavoursome.

Serves 6

6 chicken breasts
250ml whole milk
3 eggs
plain flour
250g fresh breadcrumbs
100g parmesan, finely grated
olive oil, for frying
lemon wedges, to serve

For the salsa verde
200g capers
1 bunch of mint, leaves picked
1 bunch of basil, leaves picked
6 rosemary sprigs, leaves picked
½ bunch flat-leaf parsley, leaves picked
4 garlic cloves
30g Dijon mustard
60ml red wine vinegar
10 anchovy fillets
250ml extra-virgin olive oil

For the mashed potatoes
400g potatoes, peeled and roughly chopped
   into equal-sized pieces
250ml double cream
75g unsalted butter
salt

First, prepare the salsa verde. Place all the ingredients except the oil in a pestle and mortar and grind until well combined. Transfer to a bowl, stir through the oil and set aside.

For the mashed potatoes, boil the potatoes until a skewer or knife pierces the flesh with no resistance. Drain the potatoes and allow them to steam dry.

Meanwhile, warm the cream and butter in a small saucepan and set aside. Press the potatoes through a sieve and stir through the warmed cream and butter. Season with salt to taste. Keep warm.

Meanwhile, preheat the oven to 200°C/180°C fan/Gas mark 6.

Slice the chicken breasts neatly along the length and open up like a butterfly. Place one of the breasts between two pieces of cling film or parchment paper, and bash out with a rolling pin or meat hammer until it is about 5mm thick. Repeat with the rest of the chicken breasts.

Make the schnitzel. Mix the milk and eggs in a bowl. Put some flour on one plate and combine the breadcrumbs and parmesan on another. One piece at a time, dust the chicken in the flour, dip it into the egg mixture and then dip it into the breadcrumbs, ensuring the chicken is well coated. Repeat for all the escalopes.

Heat 4–5 tablespoons of olive oil in a large frying pan on a high heat. Add the chicken escalopes (in batches, if necessary) and fry for about 2½ minutes on each side, or until golden brown all over, pressing down on the breast with a flat spatula to make sure the crust gets an even colour. Place on a baking tray.

Transfer the escalopes to the oven and cook for 5–6 minutes, until the chicken is cooked through. Serve with the warmed mash and spoon over the salsa verde.

SPICED ROAST CHICKEN
with chips & peas

A cheeky chicken dinner.

Serves 4

1.5kg whole chicken
4 garlic cloves, minced
2 teaspoons fine salt
1 teaspoon dried oregano
½ teaspoon thyme
5 tablespoons vegetable oil
2 tablespoons smoked paprika
1 tablespoon chilli powder
2 tablespoons lemon juice

For the potato wedges
100ml vegetable oil
3 large red Rooster potatoes, peeled and sliced
   into 2.5cm wedges
2 tablespoons rice flour
½ teaspoon fine salt
½ teaspoon cracked black pepper

For the peas
80g unsalted butter
1 large shallot, finely chopped
1 red chilli, deseeded and chopped
¼ teaspoon cumin seeds
350g frozen peas
juice of ½ lemon
salt

Spatchcock the chicken by removing the strip of the back bone with a sharp, strong knife. Flatten the bird with its breasts and legs facing upwards.

Mix all the remaining ingredients to create a marinade. Rub this all over the chicken, cover, and leave in the fridge for 3 hours.

Preheat the oven to 160°C/140°C fan/Gas mark 2–3.

Place the chicken flat on a roasting tray lined with baking paper and roast for 30 minutes. Then, turn up the oven to 190°C/170°C fan/Gas mark 5 and roast for a further 10 minutes, until the chicken is cooked through. Remove from the oven and allow to rest for at least 15 minutes before serving.

To prepare the wedges, pour the oil into a roasting tray large enough to comfortably fit the wedges in a single layer. Place the tray into the oven (at 190°C/170°C fan/Gas mark 5) for the oil to get hot.

Rinse the potatoes under cold water for a minute and agitate or shake them to remove any excess starch. Strain the potatoes and pat them dry with kitchen towel.

Toss the potatoes with the rice flour, salt and pepper until evenly coated, then tip the potatoes into the hot roasting tray, nudging them into a single layer. Roast for 12 minutes, then remove from the oven and carefully turn them so that another flat edge is sat in the oil. Roast for another 12–15 minutes, until glossy and crisp.

Meanwhile, prepare the peas. Melt the butter in a pan over a low heat. Sweat the shallot, chilli and cumin seeds in the butter for 2–3 minutes, or until completely tender.

Add the frozen peas to the pan, increase the heat and stir continuously for 5 minutes, until the peas are warmed through and bright green. Remove from the heat and pulse the mixture with a hand blender. Season with salt and lemon juice to taste.

Serve the chicken, wedges and peas at the table for everyone to help themselves.

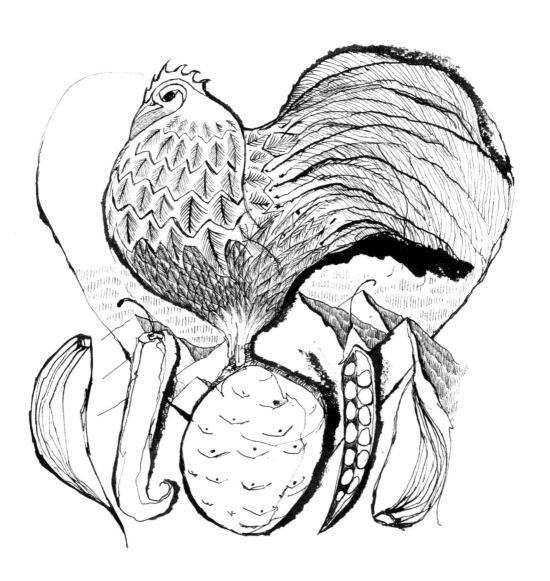

SPANISH CHICKEN CASSEROLE

During lockdown a lot of us were faced with days when there wasn't much food left in the kitchen and supermarkets were stripped bare. This recipe is so flexible, and perfect to use up any leftover vegetables that you might have in the fridge, freezer or cupboard. The warm paprika of the chorizo adds a lovely Spanish touch, with the haricot beans absorbing all of the wonderful flavours. This is a filling treat in both the summer and the winter.

Serves 4

250g dried haricot beans, soaked overnight
   in water
8 chicken thighs
2 red peppers, deseeded and diced
1 onion, sliced
1 leek, sliced
3 carrots, chopped
3 celery sticks, chopped
200g chorizo, sliced
4 garlic cloves, peeled
4 rosemary sprigs
1 small jar of artichokes in olive oil
50ml red wine vinegar
50ml Spanish olive oil
500ml chicken stock
½ bunch of flat-leaf parsley
salt and freshly ground black pepper

Preheat the oven to 180°C/160°C fan/Gas mark 4.

Drain the beans and add them to a pan with fresh water. Cook for 45–50 minutes, until tender, then drain and set aside until needed.

Heat a large frying pan on a medium heat. Add the chicken thighs and allow them to brown for 3–4 minutes, then transfer them into a casserole dish, keeping the fat that renders off in the pan, as it is full of flavour.

Add the peppers, onion, leek, carrots and celery to the frying pan, and cook for 5 minutes to colour. Transfer the vegetables to the casserole dish, along with the chorizo, garlic, rosemary and artichokes. Season well with salt and pepper.

Drizzle over the red wine vinegar and Spanish olive oil. Pour in the chicken stock and allow the liquid to come to the boil. Once boiling, transfer it to the oven and cook for 1 hour, until the chicken is cooked through and the sauce is thick.

Leave the casserole to rest for 10 minutes, then finish with flat-leaf parsley and serve.

Jamie Oliver

CORNER-SHOP CURRY SAUCE

use it your way

Who doesn't love a curry? Hero-ing store-cupboard ingredients you can pick up from your local shop, this brilliant sauce is one to use in loads of ways. I've gone for chicken curry here, but you could absolutely use salmon, white fish or prawns – just cook them through in the sauce. Or, you could choose to celebrate veggies – simply roast chunks of squash, sweet potato, cauliflower or aubergine tossed in curry paste, then add to your sauce to serve. You could even just serve the sauce as it is with rice or flat breads – winner!

Serves 4

2 x 200g free-range skinless chicken breasts
1 teaspoon jalfrezi curry paste

For the curry sauce
olive oil
2 onions, coarsely grated
2 garlic cloves, finely grated
4cm fresh ginger root, peeled and finely grated
2 red chillies, halved and deseeded (optional)
1 heaped tablespoon jalfrezi curry paste
1 heaped tablespoon mango chutney
1 x 400g tin of quality plum tomatoes
1 x 400g tin of light coconut milk
1 x 400g tin of chickpeas, drained
sea salt and freshly ground black pepper

To serve (all optional)
cooked white rice
poppadoms
little gem lettuce, sliced and dressed with
    a little lemon juice
full-fat natural yoghurt
coriander leaves, to sprinkle

For the sauce, put a large non-stick pan on a medium heat with 1 tablespoon of oil and add the grated onion, garlic and ginger, stirring regularly. Add the halved chillies and after a few minutes, once the veg has softened, stir in the curry paste, followed by the mango chutney. Cook for 2 minutes, stirring regularly.

Add the tomatoes, breaking them up with a wooden spoon and scraping up any sticky bits from the base of the pan. Simmer for a few minutes, pour in the coconut milk, then add the chickpeas. Simmer for a final 10–15 minutes, or until the consistency is to your liking. That's your corner-shop curry sauce, done.

Meanwhile, put a non-stick frying pan on a medium heat. Rub the chicken breasts with the curry paste until lightly coated, then dry fry for 6–8 minutes, or until golden and charred, turning halfway through. Remove the chicken to a board and thickly slice. If the chicken isn't cooked through at this point it's OK, because it can finish cooking in the sauce. Stir the chicken slices into the simmering sauce for the last 5 minutes, or until cooked through. Season the sauce to perfection, then serve. I like it with fluffy rice, poppadoms, shredded lemon-dressed little gem, poppadoms, a dollop of yoghurt, and a few fresh coriander leaves, if you have them.

Chef's notes...

For nutrition info, visit the recipe on jamieoliver.com

Naved Nasir

DISHOOM'S CHILLI CHICKEN

This chilli chicken recipe was inspired by an Indo-Chinese favourite from Bombay's Leopold Café. It is a much-loved café staple, but a simple and delicious one to create in your own home.

Serves 4

500g skinless chicken thighs, cut into bite-sized pieces
85g cornflour
40g strong white bread flour (plain flour will work too)
vegetable oil, for deep-frying

For the marinade
1½ tablespoons malt vinegar
1½ tablespoons dark soy sauce
1 teaspoon white pepper
pinch of salt
pinch of ajinomoto (MSG; optional)
15g coriander stalks , finely chopped
1 small egg

For the sauce
2 tablespoons vegetable oil
60g garlic, peeled weight (around 10–15 cloves), chopped
2 small red onions, finely chopped
60g fresh ginger, peeled weight, grated
60ml dark soy sauce
2 green chillies, very finely chopped
2½ tablespoons rice vinegar
pinch of ajinomoto (MSG; optional)
1 teaspoon caster sugar

To serve
2 spring onions, finely chopped
20g coriander leaves, chopped
2 green chillies, finely chopped
lime wedges

Make the marinade. In a large bowl, mix the vinegar, soy sauce, pepper, salt, ajinomoto (if using), coriander and egg.

Add the chicken pieces and toss in the marinade until evenly coated. Add the cornflour and strong flour, and mix thoroughly. Place in the fridge for at least 6 hours or ideally overnight to marinate.

When you're ready to cook, take a large, heavy-bottomed pan and heat the oil for the sauce over a medium heat. When hot, add the garlic – it should sizzle when it hits the pan – and cook until golden brown. Add the onions and ginger to the pan, stirring to avoid them sticking or burning, and fry until the onions are soft and translucent.

Add the soy sauce and cook for 2 minutes, then add the remaining sauce ingredients. Cook until the oil separates (about 10 minutes), then spoon off any excess oil. Turn down the heat just to keep the sauce warm.

Heat the vegetable oil to 160°C in a deep-fat fryer or other suitable heavy-based pan. Carefully lower the chicken into the hot oil and deep-fry for 3–4 minutes, until cooked through, crispy and golden.

Lift the chicken pieces out of the oil and drain well on kitchen paper. Add them to the sauce and toss to coat thoroughly. Serve garnished with the spring onions, coriander and chillies, and with lime wedges on the side.

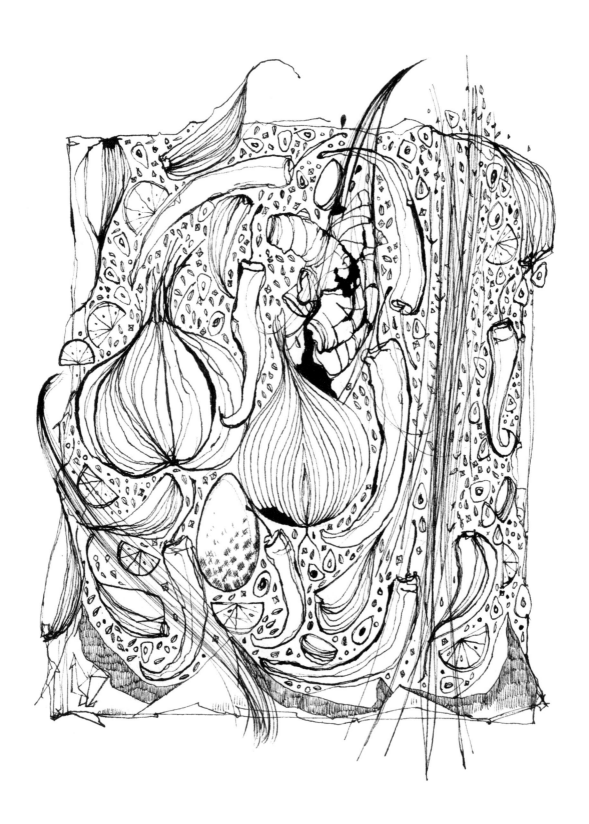

Lisa Goodwin-Allen

SPICY LAMB MEATBALLS

with three-cabbage slaw
& yoghurt pittas

*These juicy little meatballs are a crowd-pleaser.
I've given a method for cooking on a griddle pan,
but you could cook them directly on a barbecue,
if you prefer – it's how we cooked them when the
sun was shining during lockdown.*

Serves 4

40g unsalted butter
160g onion, finely chopped
4 teaspoons chaat masala
500g lean, good-quality lamb mince
110g minced pancetta
4 cloves of roasted garlic (see tip)
2 red or green chillies, deseeded and
    finely chopped
2cm fresh ginger root, peeled and grated
1 teaspoon salt
olive oil, to drizzle

For the yoghurt pittas
300g self-raising flour
200g full-fat natural yoghurt
2 teaspoons nigella seeds
good pinch of salt
about 1 tablespoon sunflower oil

For the three-cabbage slaw
¼ red cabbage, finely sliced
¼ white cabbage, finely sliced
¼ sweetheart cabbage, finely sliced
1 carrot, peeled and finely sliced
1 red onion, finely sliced
100g good-quality mayonnaise
100g crème fraîche
juice and finely grated zest of 1 lime
15g coriander, leaves and stems chopped
salt, to taste

Melt the butter in a medium pan over a medium heat.
When hot, add the onion and chaat masala, then cook
for 3–5 minutes, until the onions are soft. Remove from
the pan and leave to cool.

Place the lamb mince into a large mixing bowl and
add the cooled onions, minced pancetta, roasted
garlic, and the chilli, ginger root and salt. Mix well until
combined. Divide the mixture into 12 equal-sized balls.
Place these on a tray and refrigerate for at least
30 minutes to firm up.

Meanwhile, prepare the pittas. In a large bowl
combine the flour, yoghurt, nigella seeds and salt. Mix
well and bring the ingredients together to form a dough.
Transfer the dough to a clean surface and knead it for
4–5 minutes, until smooth. Then, lightly wrap the dough
in cling film and leave it to rest for 15 minutes.

Make the slaw. Mix together the cabbages, carrot and
red onion in a large bowl. Add the mayonnaise, crème
fraîche and lime juice and zest and mix well to combine.
Add the chopped coriander, mix lightly, then season with
salt to taste. Refrigerate until you're ready to serve.

To prepare the roasted garlic mayonnaise, place all the
ingredients in a bowl and, using a hand blender, blitz until
smooth. Refrigerate until you're ready to serve.

Heat a griddle to hot. Remove the meatballs from the
fridge and lightly drizzle a small amount of olive oil over
each one.

Place the meatballs on to the hot griddle, then reduce
the heat to medium and cook for 8–10 minutes, turning
every 1–2 minutes, until the meatballs are just cooked
through in the middle and lovely and charred on the
outsides. Remove from the heat and transfer to a plate
to rest.

For the roasted garlic mayonnaise
200g mayonnaise
100g crème fraîche
3 cloves of roasted garlic
2 tablespoons good-quality chicken stock
   (ideally homemade)
good pinch of salt

While the meatballs are resting, quickly cook the pittas. Heat a griddle or a large non-stick frying pan until hot. Remove the dough from the cling film and cut it into 8 equal-sized balls.

Lightly oil a clean work surface and rolling pin. One piece at a time, place the dough on to the oiled surface and rub a small amount of oil on top. Roll it out to a circle 2mm thick.

Place the pitta on the griddle or in the hot frying pan on a medium heat and cook for 1½ minutes on each side, until lightly golden and soft enough to fold easily. Repeat to cook all the pittas, then serve with the meatballs, slaw and roasted garlic mayo.

Chef's notes...

To roast your own garlic bulb, place the whole bulb on a roasting tray and drizzle with oil. Roast at 200°C/180°C fan /Gas mark 6 for 10–15 minutes.

Elizabeth Haigh

LAMB PASTINI
with parmesan salad

Orzo or 'pastini' (rice-shaped) pasta is a store-cupboard staple in this household, because my son, Riley, absolutely loves rice – but making rice every day for work means that I always crave some carby pasta. This is a good compromise. The rich fattiness from the lamb, which you can easily substitute with leftover lamb from a roast, marries perfectly with parmesan. You can add any vegetables (I like spinach) into the bake, but I'm dealing with a fussy toddler, who can spot vegetables a mile off, so we always pair this with a salad that the adults can eat on the side.

Serves 4

2 tablespoons vegetable oil
300g lamb shoulder, boneless and diced
   (or lamb breast, leg or even leftover
   cooked lamb)
1 small onion or 1 shallot, finely diced
1 garlic clove, crushed
50g unsalted butter
2 anchovies, in olive oil, finely chopped
500ml boiling water from a kettle
1 tablespoon vegetable bouillon powder
2 tablespoons tomato purée
500g orzo
salt and freshly ground black pepper
plenty of parmesan, finely grated, to serve
dressed salad leaves, to serve

Preheat the oven to 180°C/160°C fan/Gas mark 4. You'll need an ovenproof dish about 30cm wide and 6cm deep.

Pour the oil into a casserole dish or large frying pan on a medium heat. When hot, add the lamb in batches, browning it on all sides, and setting each batch aside on a plate to rest while you brown the next. Keep going until all the lamb pieces are well coloured. Take care not to overcrowd the pan. Set aside.

Add the onion or shallot and the garlic to the hot pan and sauté for about 5–7 minutes, until soft and golden. Add the lamb back to the pan along with the resting juices, butter and anchovies, and stir well. Season to taste, then tip everything into the baking dish.

Pour the boiling water into a jug, then stir in the bouillon and tomato purée. Pour the liquid over the lamb mixture.

Scatter the orzo slowly and evenly over the mixture in the dish, then use a wooden spoon to push the orzo into the lamb mixture, so that it's covered with the stock liquid.

Cover the tray tightly with foil, then place in the oven on the top shelf to bake for 30 minutes.

After 30 minutes, gently lift one corner of the foil to check the bake. If it still looks quite wet, cover it again and cook it for another 5 minutes, until the pasta has absorbed most of the stock. Then remove the foil and ruffle the pasta with a large spoon or fork. Bake, uncovered, for another 5 minutes, until there's no liquid left, the orzo is cooked and there's a lovely golden, crispy top.

Remove the bake from the oven and serve with plenty of grated parmesan and a dressed salad, preferably with lots of lemon juice and good-quality olive oil.

Nokx Majozi

LAMB BUNNY CHOW

This classic South African recipe is a family favourite. It's great served with a tomato and onion salad.

Serves 4

40ml vegetable oil
1 onion, chopped
1 bay leaf
2 cinnamon sticks
1 teaspoon fennel seeds
1½ tablespoons ginger and garlic paste
1 teaspoon masala curry powder
1 teaspoon garam masala
1 teaspoon ground turmeric
500g lamb shoulder, diced
1 x 400g tin of chopped tomatoes
2 potatoes, peeled and cubed
1 large loaf of unsliced bread, or 4 round
    bread rolls
salt and freshly ground black pepper
coriander sprig, leaves picked, to garnish

Heat the oil in a large saucepan over a medium heat. Add the onion, bay leaf, cinnamon sticks and fennel seeds and cook for about 8–10 minutes, stirring, until the onions are softened and translucent. Add the ginger and garlic paste, masala curry powder, garam masala and turmeric and mix well.

Add the meat and turn to coat evenly in the spiced onion mixture. Cook for 5 minutes, until browned, then add the tomatoes. If the pan looks a little dry, you can add 150ml of water at this point too. Braise over a low heat for 30 minutes, stirring from time to time. Then, add the potatoes and 100ml of water and cook until the potatoes and meat are tender. Season to taste.

To assemble, cut the bread into quarters (or, if you are using individual rolls, cut off the tops). Hollow out the inners, keeping the crust intact, and scoop the meat and potato into the hollow. Garnish with coriander leaves to serve.

Chef's notes...

If you have leftover filling, it can be kept in the fridge and enjoyed the next day with rice or salad – it tastes even better!

LAMB BOULANGÈRE
with vegetables – family-style

The juices from this slowly roasted shoulder of lamb drip on to potatoes and onions to create hearty rich flavours, served with an unctuous red wine gravy. A real comforting family feast for all!

Serves 6

3kg bone-in lamb shoulder
olive oil
a few rosemary sprigs, leaves picked
2kg large waxy potatoes, peeled and
 thinly sliced
3 large red onions, thinly sliced
bunch of thyme, leaves picked
5 garlic cloves, chopped
570ml good-quality chicken stock
 (preferably homemade)
unsalted butter, for greasing
sea salt and freshly ground black pepper
mint sauce, to serve

For the red wine sauce
2–3 tablespoons vegetable oil
1 onion, sliced
1 carrot, peeled and sliced
1 celery stick, sliced
2 garlic cloves, smashed with the handle
 of a knife
½ teaspoon salt
1 teaspoon tomato purée
250ml red wine
570ml chicken stock (preferably homemade
 or made with a good-quality stock cube)
½ bunch of thyme sprigs
100g unsalted butter, diced
1 teaspoon red wine vinegar

For the vegetables
2 carrots, roughly chopped
1 large turnip, peeled and roughly chopped to
 the same size pieces as the carrots
1 bunch of baby leeks, trimmed
1 bunch of baby red beetroots, trimmed
80g unsalted butter

Make sure the lamb is at room temperature before you begin. Place the lamb on a large plate or board and drizzle with olive oil. Sprinkle with the rosemary leaves and season well. Set aside. Preheat the oven to 150°C/130°C fan/Gas Mark 2.

In a bowl, combine the potatoes, onions, thyme, garlic and chicken stock. Season well with salt and pepper.

Use a little butter to grease a roasting tin, then spread the potato mixture over the tray in an even layer. Place the lamb on top.

Cover with some baking paper, then encase the lamb and potatoes with foil. Transfer to the oven and cook for 4½ hours, removing the covering in the last hour, until the lamb has taken on some colour without drying out.

Towards the end of the lamb's cooking time, make the red wine sauce. Heat the vegetable oil in a frying pan and add the onion, carrot, celery and garlic. Cook until the vegetables are nicely caramelised, then add the salt and tomato purée and deglaze the pan with the wine. Cook until the wine has evaporated, then add the stock and thyme. Simmer for 30 minutes, then strain through a sieve and discard the vegetables.

Put the liquid back into the pan and reduce by half, then add the butter and red wine vinegar. Simmer until the sauce becomes glossy and thick enough to coat the back of a spoon. Cover and keep warm until you're ready to serve.

Remove the lamb from the oven, cover again and rest somewhere warm for 45 minutes.

While the meat is resting, bring a large pan of salted water to the boil (you want about 600ml of water with 1 tablespoon of salt added). Add the vegetables and butter and cook them for about 10 minutes, until tender.

Flash the lamb through a hot oven to reheat and serve family-style at the table. Arrange the vegetables on a platter with a jug of red wine sauce and plenty of mint sauce on the side. Enjoy!

LAMB KOFTAS
with tzatziki

This is a great recipe for barbecuing or grilling and can be enjoyed informally as part of a meal or as suggested with servings of pitta, hummus, peppers and tzatziki.

I have always been fascinated with North African cuisine, and the lovely mix of spices and herbs which really do accentuate this dish's flavours.

Serves 4

olive oil, for frying
1 red onion, halved and each half sliced
    into wedges
1 red pepper, deseeded and cut into strips
salt and freshly ground black pepper
pitta breads, to serve
hummus, to serve

For the lamb koftas
400g lamb shoulder, minced
¼ small red onion, chopped
1 tablespoon chopped flat-leaf parsley (leaves
    and stalks)
1 tablespoon chopped mint leaves
½ tablespoon ground cumin
½ tablespoon ras el hanout
1 garlic clove, crushed or grated
½ red chilli, deseeded and finely diced
pinch of salt

For the tzatziki
300g Greek yoghurt
½ cucumber, halved lengthways, deseeded
    and grated
½ garlic clove, crushed or grated
juice of ½ lemon

You will need
8 long bamboo skewers soaked in water for
    at least 30 minutes

First, make the koftas. Place the mince in a bowl and add the remaining ingredients. Mix well to combine. Take a little of the mixture and pan-fry it over a medium heat until cooked, then taste and check the seasoning – adjusting if necessary.

Divide the mixture into 8 equal pieces, then mould each piece into a long sausage shape. Skewer each sausage on to a bamboo skewer and place on a tray. Cover with cling film and refrigerate to rest and firm up for 30 minutes.

Prepare your barbecue for cooking, or, heat a griddle pan to hot.

Meanwhile, prepare the tzatziki. Mix all the ingredients together and season with salt. Transfer to a small serving bowl, cover and place in the fridge until you're ready to serve.

Heat a drizzle of oil in a pan over a medium heat. Add the onion wedges and the slices of pepper, season with salt and pepper and fry for about 10 minutes, until softened. Set aside and keep warm.

When you're ready to serve, remove the koftas from the fridge and drizzle them with a little olive oil. Place them on to the barbecue grill, or into the griddle pan, and cook for about 10 minutes, turning regularly, until cooked through and coloured all over. Place the pitta breads on to the grill or griddle pan to heat through.

Serve the koftas with the warmed pittas, hummus, softened onions and pepper and a generous helping of tzatziki.

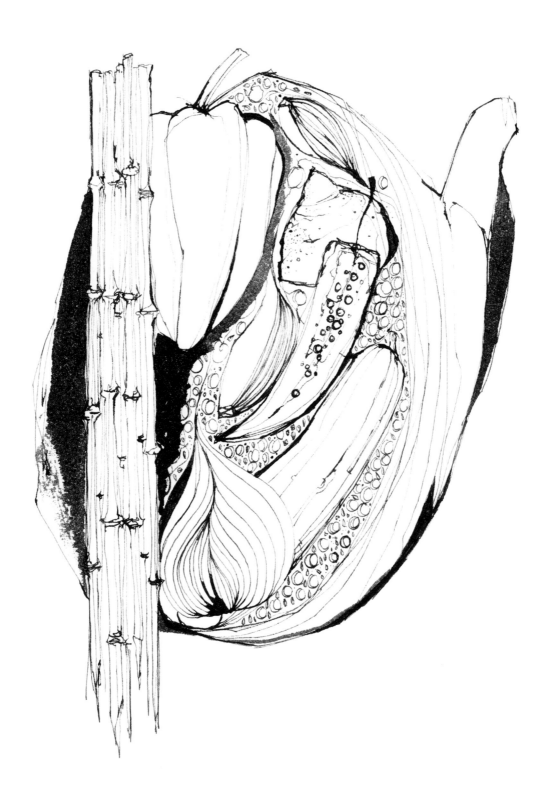

GALVIN BROTHERS' BURGER

This classic burger recipe is a firm favourite for both me and my brother Jeff, and often features on our menus, both at home and in the restaurants. We regularly mix up the sides and garnishes, but this is one of my favourite combinations.

Serves 4

For the tomato jam
1 tablespoon olive oil
½ Spanish onion, finely chopped
1 garlic clove, crushed
pinch of smoked paprika
20ml white wine vinegar
1 tablespoon tomato purée
20g smoked sundried tomato, chopped
1 x 400g tin of chopped tomatoes
1 teaspoon demerara sugar
salt and freshly ground black pepper

For the burgers
350g chuck steak, diced and chilled
175g flank steak, diced and chilled
175g fat from aged beef sirloin or from
    around a fillet

For the quick pickled cucumber
½ small cucumber, sliced into ribbons
1–2 tablespoons cider vinegar
1 teaspoon caster sugar
pinch of salt

To finish
¼ iceberg lettuce, finely shredded
dressing of 80g mayonnaise mixed with
    2 tablespoons grain mustard
4 slices smoked cheddar (I use
    Applewood cheddar)
4 brioche buns, halved
skin-on fries, to serve

First, prepare the tomato jam. Heat the oil in a frying pan over a medium–low heat. Add the onion and sweat for about 8–10 minutes, until golden. Add the garlic and smoked paprika and cook for 3–4 minutes, until the garlic has softened. Add the vinegar and allow to bubble. Add the rest of the ingredients and cook very slowly for about 25 minutes, until thick, then season to taste, allow to cool and keep in the fridge until needed. (This will make more than you need, but it will store in a sterilised jar in the fridge for up to 1 month.)

Make the burgers. Put all the meat and fat into the bowl of a stand mixer fitted with the hook or beater attachment. Season with salt and pepper and combine on medium speed for 30 seconds–1 minute, until the meats have just come together. (Or use your hands to bring it together until just combined.) Remove the meat mixture from the bowl, wrap it in cling film and allow it to rest for 15 minutes.

Take a small walnut-sized ball of the mixture and pan fry it over a medium heat until cooked to taste; check the seasoning, adjusting as necessary. Divide the mixture into 4 equal pieces and shape into patties, each of about 175g. Set aside.

Dress the iceberg lettuce with the grain dressing and set aside.

Heat a griddle pan to hot. Add the burgers and cook until they are cooked through and the internal temperature reaches 71°C when probed with a thermometer. Top each with a slice of cheddar, cover with a cloche if you have one and leave to melt (the cheese will melt without the cloche, it will just take a bit longer).

Meanwhile, combine all the ingredients for the pickled cucumber and set aside. Toast the burger buns, then spread some of the tomato jam on each base. Place the dressed lettuce on top of the tomato jam. When the burgers are ready, top the lettuce with a burger and then a few ribbons of pickled cucumber. Finish with the bun lid. Secure with a skewer and serve with fries on the side.

Phil Howard

CHARGRILLED BEEF RUMP

with a feast of onions, field mushrooms,
garlic & potatoes

*Lockdown for me was about cooking great,
great food with minimal fuss and time – quick
and forgiving food that delivered in spades. This
recipe is big, ballsy stuff when your hunger and
desire to impress outplays your appetite to get
bogged down in the kitchen with the fiddly stuff.
It is a feast ... of well-roasted rump of beef and
a collection of very primal and visual garnishes.
These are simple things that need some good
old-fashioned love and care, but if cooked with
passion and understanding will seduce any
gathering of like-minded food fiends. This is
about caramelisation and deep, mellow flavours.
Control the heat to ensure you get rich, golden
colours that pack a mighty punch.*

*You need to make sure that the beef is at room
temperature, so remove it from the fridge around
2 hours before you intend to cook it.*

Serves 6

12 potatoes, 8–10cm long
100ml vegetable oil, plus extra for brushing
6 onions
150g unsalted butter
6 plump garlic bulbs
10 large field mushrooms, peeled
2 large banana shallots, finely diced
1 thyme sprig, leaves picked
200ml double cream
80g fresh or dried white breadcrumbs
15g flat-leaf parsley leaves
1kg beef rump cap, with good fat cover,
    at room temperature
1 tablespoon dripping
12 cavolo nero leaves
salt and freshly ground black pepper

Preheat the oven to 180°C/160°C fan/Gas mark 4.

The potatoes need to be scalloped, with slices from
one end to the other that go nearly, but not completely,
through the potato. One by one, place the potatoes on a
chopping board with a chopstick (or similar) either side.
This will prevent you from cutting right through. Leaving
1cm at each end uncut, use a small, sharp knife to cut
slices into the potatoes at 2mm intervals all the way
along. Transfer the potatoes to a small ovenproof tray,
brush them with a little vegetable oil, add 20ml of the oil
to the tray, season lightly with salt (they get seasoned
again) and bake, basting every 10 minutes, for
40–45 minutes, until golden brown. Remove them from
the oven, sprinkle again with a bit more salt and set aside.

Reduce the oven to 160°C/140°C fan/Gas mark 3.

Without peeling, cut the onions in half horizontally (not
through the root). Place a heavy-based, ovenproof pan
over a high heat, add 25ml of vegetable oil, sprinkle the
surface of the pan with salt and place the onion halves
into the pan, cut-side downwards. Cook over a high heat
for about 3–4 minutes, until they are golden. Add about
20g of butter and cook for a little longer, until the onions
are a rich golden-brown colour, then transfer the pan
to the oven and bake the onions for 30 minutes, or until
they are completely tender. Set aside.

Meanwhile, prepare the garlic. Cut the top one third
off the top of each garlic bulb. Place a heavy-based,
ovenproof pan over a medium heat. Once hot, add 25ml
of the vegetable oil and another 20g of the butter and
allow to heat up and the butter to melt. Season with salt
and place the garlic bulbs, cut-side downwards, into the
pan. Cook until just golden and then transfer to the oven
to bake for 20 minutes, until the garlic is soft, tender and
wonderfully mellow. Set aside, but leave the oven on.

While the onions and garlic are baking, prepare the
mushrooms. Cut the mushroom stalks so that they
are flush with the gills. Dice 4 of the mushrooms into
roughly 5mm cubes. Melt a further 20g of the butter in
a heavy-based pan, add the shallots, a pinch of salt

and the thyme leaves. Sweat the shallots for a few minutes, until translucent. Add the diced mushrooms, another pinch of salt and cook for a further 3–4 minutes, until softened. Add the cream and cook until the cream has bound to the mushrooms and the mixture is rich. Check the seasoning and set aside.

Heat a medium-sized frying pan over a medium heat. Add the remaining oil and season the base of the pan with salt. Place the 6 remaining field mushrooms into the pan, season with a little more salt and cook for a minute or so or until the bases have coloured a bit. Add the remaining butter to the pan and allow to sizzle for a minute or so. Add a splash of water, cover with a lid and cook for 2–3 minutes, until tender. Remove the lid, allow the water to cook away and set aside to cool.

Whizz the crumbs, parsley and a pinch of salt in a blender until you have green breadcrumbs. Tip them out on to a plate and set aside.

Place the 6 cooled mushrooms in a baking dish, tops downwards. Spoon the creamy mushroom mixture into the caps and top with the parsley crumb. Bake the mushrooms for 20 minutes, or until the crumb has caught some colour. Keep warm while you cook the beef.

Reduce the oven heat to 130°C/110°C fan/Gas mark 1. Place a large, heavy-based pan over a medium heat and allow it to heat up for 1 minute. Season the room-temperature beef generously with salt and pepper. Add the dripping to a pan and allow it to melt, then place the rump into the pan too. Turn the heat down if it seems too high – the aim is to slowly render and caramelise the beef fat so that the fat layer is crisp, golden brown and utterly delicious! This should take a good 5 or so minutes. Once coloured, turn up the heat and flip the beef over. Seal it for a minute or two, until the meat is coloured.

Transfer the beef to the oven and cook it for about 30 minutes, until medium rare. Remove it from the oven and set it aside to rest. Increase the oven to 160°C/140°C fan/Gas mark 2–3.

Blanch the cavolo nero in a large pan of heavily salted water for 1 minute. Warm through the beef and other vegetables by passing them through the warm oven for about 10 minutes. Carve the beef into slices, drizzle with its roasting juices, and season with a few flakes of sea salt. Serve it with everything carefully and generously arranged on a large wooden board.

Thomasina Miers

STEAK & CHEESE TACOS

This is a classic taco in Mexico which can be made with any cut of meat, depending on the occasion. Skirt steak is great for flavour and budget, but you have to cook it right; rib-eye is for high days and holidays and my favourite; and sirloin is for those that like a smooth bite.

Given what we know about climate change, buy grass-fed beef from cows that have been reared outdoors. Industrial meat farming is a huge contributor to greenhouse gases, so I try to support farmers who are protecting biodiversity and sequestering carbon. Less meat, better quality is my mantra and support your local farmer!

Serves 4

2 garlic cloves, unpeeled
good pinch of dried oregano, preferably Mexican
½ teaspoon sea salt, plus extra to season
juice and finely grated zest of 1 unwaxed orange
3 tablespoons olive oil
350g rib-eye, sirloin or skirt steaks
1 bunch of spring onions, trimmed and outer
    leaves discarded
freshly ground black pepper

For the salsa
3 large, ripe plum tomatoes
1 small red onion, cut into wedges
2 garlic cloves
½ teaspoon sea salt
1 chipotle chilli
handful of coriander, leaves and
    stalks separated
juice of 2 limes
pinch of caster sugar, if needed

To serve
good-quality hard cheese, grated
corn or flour tortillas, warmed
refried beans
radishes or meat radishes, thinly sliced
1 avocado, destoned and sliced
lime wedges

Bash the garlic and oregano together with the salt and some freshly ground black pepper. Add the orange zest and thin down the marinade with 1 teaspoon of orange juice and 1 tablespoon of the olive oil. Rub the marinade over the steak and leave to season for 30 minutes at room temperature, or for a few hours (or overnight) in the fridge.

To make the salsa, heat a large, heavy-based frying pan over a high heat. Dry-roast the tomatoes in the pan for about 15 minutes, until blackened all over. Remove from the pan and set aside. Repeat for the onion and garlic, cooking for about 10 minutes, until the garlic is soft.

Put the onion and garlic into a pestle and mortar with the salt and the whole chipotle and pound vigorously. Finely chop the coriander stalks and add these to the mortar along with the blackened tomatoes and work the mixture to a salsa. Add the lime juice, then also add a pinch of sugar if the tomatoes are poor.

Remove the steaks from the fridge at least 30 minutes before you intend to cook. Heat a large, heavy-based frying pan or griddle over a high heat and, when smoking hot, add the steaks to the pan. Sear for 2–3 minutes on each side, depending on thickness, until pink and juicy in the middle (otherwise it will be tough to eat). Rest the steaks on a chopping board for at least 5 minutes before slicing.

While the steak is resting, rub the spring onions in a little of the remaining oil and season well. Griddle for about 4–5 minutes, until soft and slightly charred.

Slice the steak into very thin slivers across the grain of the meat. (You can check this by seeing which way the 'threads' of the meat run and cut against them rather than along them; this will make the texture much better.)

Wipe out the frying-pan and toast small piles of grated cheese for 2–3 minutes until golden, to make 'chicharron' de queso – cheese scratchings. Serve the steak in warmed tortillas with the charred spring onions, toasted cheese, salsa, refried beans, radishes and slices of avocado, scattered with coriander leaves. Hand around lime wedges and plenty of napkins!

Daniel Clifford

STEAK & CHIPS
with Béarnaise sauce

You can't beat a steak and chips. I cooked this with my family throughout lockdown until the kids absolutely mastered it! The recipe will give you too much Béarnaise reduction for just two steaks, but I like to make it and keep some in a jar in the fridge – it will keep for up to 1 month. The shallots are great in a cheese sandwich.

Serves 2

150g unsalted butter
3 garlic cloves
3 lemon thyme sprigs
2 dry-aged, thick-cut rib-eye steaks (I get
    mine from R & J Yorkshire Butchers), at
    room temperature
Maldon sea salt

For the chips
6 large Koffmann chipping potatoes, peeled
    and chipped
1 tablespoon salt
vegetable oil, for deep-frying
beef dripping, for deep-frying

For the Béarnaise reduction
400ml white wine
200ml white wine vinegar
½ shallot, finely sliced
1 black peppercorn
3 tarragon sprigs

For the Béarnaise sauce
2 egg yolks
2 tablespoons Béarnaise reduction
125g light nut-brown butter, at
    room temperature
splash of lemon juice

Wash the chips under running water, until the water runs clear. Place the chips in a large pan with the salt, cover with water and bring to the boil. Reduce the heat to a simmer and cook for about 10–15 minutes, until the potatoes are just cooked and still holding their shape. Drain and lay on a cooling rack to cool completely.

Fill a deep-fat fryer with the vegetable oil and beef dripping and allow it to come up to 160°C on the fryer thermometer. Place the chips into the fat and fry for 4 minutes, until golden. Remove from the fryer and set aside to drain on kitchen paper. Reserve the fat pan for when you're ready to cook the chips fully to serve.

Place all the ingredients for the Béarnaise reduction into a pan and gently cook until it has reduced by half (about 2–4 minutes). Remove from the heat.

Make the Béarnaise sauce. Set a pan of water over a medium heat and bring it up to a simmer. Place the egg yolks in a heatproof bowl. Add the 2 tablespoons of the reduction and 1 tablespoon of water and set the bowl over the pan, reducing the heat so that the water gently simmers. Whisk the mixture in the bowl until thick and pale in colour. Then slowly add the nut-brown butter to the egg yolks; if it gets too thick add a little water – you're looking for the consistency of mayonnaise.

Put a good splash of lemon juice in a pan with a good pinch of salt. Bring to the boil to dissolve the salt, then add this to the sauce, taste and adjust the seasoning if needed. Keep warm.

When you're ready to serve, heat the fat in the chip pan to 190°C. Add the chips to the pan and fry for about 90 seconds, or until golden brown.

Meanwhile, heat a frying pan over a high heat until it's very hot. Add a little of the butter, then the garlic and thyme. Add the steaks and fry for 1 minute on one side, to colour, then turn them over, season with salt and colour the other side for a further minute. Repeat, adding a little more butter, turning the steaks every 30 seconds until done to your liking. Rest the steaks for 10 minutes and serve with the chips and sauce.

BEER-BRAISED BRISKET MAC 'N' CHEESE

This recipe is special to me because when we launched our delivery service, Made In Oldstead, during lockdown, it was one of the first dishes we made. It may be a far cry from what I usually cook at The Black Swan, but it's comfort in a bowl. I love to use a chocolate-y porter from a local brewery, Treboom. Cheese-wise, I love trying out different types from our friends at The Courtyard Dairy whenever I make mac 'n' cheese. A combination of Summerfield Alpine, Hafod and Ogleshield is an absolute winner.

Serves 4 with plenty of leftovers

For the brisket
2 teaspoons salt
2 teaspoons cracked black pepper
2 teaspoons garlic powder
2 teaspoons onion powder
2 teaspoons sweet paprika
1kg beef brisket
2 tablespoons olive oil
200ml beef stock
400ml bottle dark beer, stout or porter
1 tablespoon light brown soft sugar
1 tablespoon Henderson's relish
2 garlic cloves, crushed
2 bay leaves
handful thyme sprigs

For the mac 'n' cheese
100g unsalted butter
100g plain flour
500–750ml whole milk (depending on how thick you want your sauce)
100ml double cream
250g cheddar
50g parmesan
100g mozzarella
1 tablespoon Dijon mustard
1 tablespoon Henderson's relish
250g cooked macaroni (about 125g uncooked)
salt and freshly ground black pepper

Preheat the oven to 150°C/130°C fan/Gas mark 2. Prepare the brisket. Combine the salt, pepper, garlic and onion powders and paprika in a bowl, then rub the mixture generously over the brisket. Heat the oil in a large heavy-bottomed casserole dish. Add the brisket and brown it on all sides (about 2–3 minutes each side). Keep turning it until it's browned all over.

Pour the beef stock and beer over the brisket, then add the sugar, relish, garlic, bay and thyme. Bring the liquid to the boil, put the lid on the casserole dish and place it in the oven for 3–3½ hours, basting now and again, until the meat comes away easily and is string-like when you pull. Check the liquid from time to time and add a little water if it reduces too much.

Remove the brisket from the oven, carefully transfer it to a plate and cover with foil. Strain the cooking juices through a sieve into a clean pan. Bring the juices to the boil, then reduce them down so that you have a sauce that is thick enough to coat the back of a spoon.

Once your brisket is nicely rested, which will take about 20 minutes, carefully shred it with two forks and pour over your thickened sauce. Set the meat aside and increase the oven to 200°C/180°C fan/Gas mark 6.

Now it's time to make your mac 'n' cheese. Melt the butter in a large saucepan over a medium heat. Add the flour and cook for 3–5 minutes, until the mixture begins to darken and smells slightly nutty. Gradually add the milk, stirring continuously until the mixture begins to turn into a thick sauce. Add the double cream, 200g of the cheddar, all the parmesan and mozzarella, the mustard and Henderson's relish. Season with salt and pepper and stir until the cheese has fully melted.

Add the cooked macaroni and stir carefully until the pasta is fully coated in the sauce. Transfer the macaroni cheese to a large ovenproof serving dish. Sprinkle the reserved 50g of cheddar on top, then pile the brisket on top of that. Warm through in the oven for 5 minutes to crisp up. Serve with a cold bottle of the beer you used in the brisket, for the perfect pairing.

Anna Haugh

BLACK PUDDING BURGER
with cumin & chilli wedges

If you don't think you're a fan of black pudding, think again. Whilst black pudding may be a controversial ingredient, my tasty burger patties are packed full of flavour. Served with crispy potato wedges, ketchup and your favourite chilli sauce, this is one burger and chips you'll really want to sink your teeth into.

Serves 4

For the wedges
800g King Edward potatoes, skin on
2 teaspoons salt
1 pinch of chilli powder
1 teaspoon ground cumin
2–2½ tablespoons vegetable oil

For the burger
200g black pudding
350g minced beef (10% fat)
1–2 pinches of salt
1 egg yolk
1 tablespoon vegetable oil, for frying

To serve
3 tablespoons ketchup
4 large baby gem leaves
4 burger buns, sliced in half
1 teaspoon Tabasco, or your favourite
   chilli sauce

Preheat the oven to 200°C/180°C fan/Gas mark 6.

Cut your potatoes into 2–3cm pieces, and place them in a bowl with the salt, chilli powder, cumin and oil. Give everything a good mix. Spread the wedges equally between 2 baking trays and bake for about 30 minutes. Check the potato wedges are cooked all the way through by breaking one in half. If it's not soft and fluffy on the inside cook for another 5–10 minutes. They should be crispy and golden.

Meanwhile, make the burgers. Crumble the black pudding into the mince, add the salt and egg yolk and mix well with clean hands. Roll into a large ball, cut that ball into quarters, then shape each quarter into a burger patty.

Add the oil to a large frying pan set over a high heat. When the pan is hot, sprinkle a little extra salt on the burgers and place them in the pan. Leave for 2 minutes, until golden brown on the undersides, then turn over and cook for another 3 minutes, until browned all over and cooked through.

Turn off the heat and leave the burgers to rest in the pan. Meanwhile, add ketchup and lettuce equally to the base of each burger bun. Top with the burgers and sprinkle with a little of the Tabasco or favourite chilli sauce. Finish off with the bun lid and serve immediately with the wedges alongside.

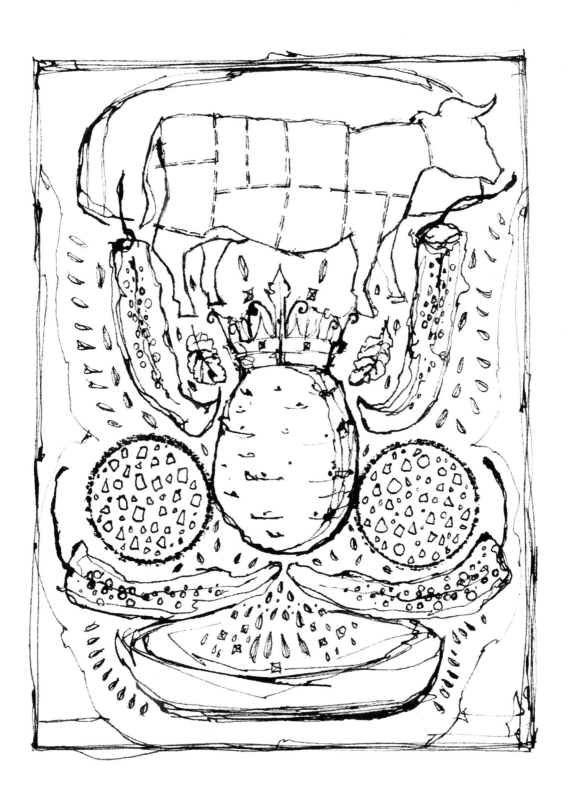

Calum Franklin

PORK & BLACK PUDDING PIESOLATION

This was the first large pie I baked at home during lockdown, and it was a gift for an industry friend who lives locally who had sent me a lovely package of food. It will always remind me of the community spirit we saw blossom at the beginning of all this, friends helping each other, building relationships with our neighbours and making time to reconnect with each other despite the physical barrier.

Serves 10

500g plain flour, plus extra for dusting
2 teaspoons salt
250g unsalted butter, cut into 2cm cubes
 and chilled, plus extra for greasing the tin
2 eggs, beaten
60ml ice-cold water
2 egg yolks, beaten with 1 teaspoon water,
 to form a wash

For the filling
300g black pudding
800g pork shoulder, half coarsely minced,
 half diced into 3cm cubes
300g smoked, sweet-cured streaky bacon,
 roughly chopped
100g pork back fat, diced into 2cm cubes (you
 can use an extra 50g pork shoulder and 50g
 bacon if you cannot source it)
2 teaspoons fennel seeds
2 teaspoons yellow mustard seeds
2 teaspoons fine table salt
30g sage leaves, finely chopped
1 teaspoon coarsely ground black pepper

For the jelly
6 bronze gelatine leaves
300ml chicken stock
100ml dry cider
4 sage sprigs

To make the pastry dough, put the flour, salt and butter in a large mixing bowl and rub together with your fingertips until you achieve a rough breadcrumb consistency. Put the beaten eggs in a separate bowl and add the ice-cold water. Whisk until well combined, then pour the mixture into the dry ingredients and knead them together into a rough dough.

Tip out the dough on to a lightly floured work surface and knead a few more times until the ingredients are combined, but take care not to over-work. Break off one third of the dough, form it into a ball, wrap it in cling film and flatten it slightly. Do the same with the larger portion of dough, then put both portions into the fridge to chill for 20 minutes.

Make the filling. Peel any casing off the black pudding and crumble it into a bowl, then gently massage it back together until it becomes malleable. Roll it into a hockey-puck shape, then place it between two sheets of greaseproof paper. Using a rolling pin, roll the black pudding into a 20cm diameter circle. Transfer it to a flat tray and place it in the freezer.

Grease the inside of a 23cm non-stick springform cake tin with the softened butter. Take the larger portion of dough from the fridge and let it sit for a few minutes before unwrapping it and dusting it with a little flour. Roll it out to a large circle about 5mm thick. Fold the circle in half and then again into a quarter and transfer it to the cake tin. Unfold the circle inside the cake tin and, working quickly, line the inside of the tin, gently pushing the dough into the corners and sides. You will be left with a pastry overhang on the top of the tin. Trim this to 3cm with a pair of scissors (keep the trimmings). Place the whole tin in the freezer to chill for 10 minutes, or if it doesn't fit, place it in the fridge for 25 minutes.

Roll the remaining third of dough to a circle, roughly 26cm in diameter (slightly wider than the cake tin), again 5mm thick. Line a baking tray with baking paper and transfer the pastry disc to it, along with the reserved pastry trimmings, then place the tray in the fridge.

Put the remaining filling ingredients in a large mixing bowl and mix until well combined. Weigh the mixture and divide it in half. Remove the cake tin from the freezer and stuff the pastry case with one half of the pork mixture. Flatten the mixture well. Peel the greaseproof paper from the black pudding and sit the disc of black pudding on top of the layer of pork filling. Top with the remaining half of the pork mixture, flattening it out to fill the pie case in an even layer.

Remove the pastry lid from the fridge and lay it across the top of the pie. Brush the top with a thin coating of egg wash. When both the overhanging pastry from the base and the lid are supple enough to work, crimp them together on to the top edge of the pie. Try not to leave the crimping hanging outside the edge of the cake tin or the pie will be difficult to remove after cooking.

Roll out the pastry trimmings and use them to cut out letters for decoration (P-I-E-S-O-L-A-T-I-O-N) and place these on top of the pie. Cut a small hole into the centre of the lid to allow steam to escape. Make a little chimney tube out of tin foil, about 5cm in height (roll it around a marker pen for shape) and fit it into the steam hole. Place the pie in the fridge to cool for 20 minutes, then remove it and give it a second egg wash all over.

While the pie is chilling, preheat the oven to 180°C/160°C fan/Gas mark 4. Bake the pie for about 50–60 minutes, or until a meat thermometer inserted into the centre of the pie reaches 55°C. Remove from the oven and allow to cool overnight.

To make the jelly, soak the gelatine in cold water for 3 minutes to soften. Meanwhile, pour the chicken stock and cider into a small pan, add the sprigs of sage, and warm the mixture through over a medium heat. When the gelatine is softened, remove it from the water and squeeze out the excess. Remove the stock mixture from the heat and add the gelatine leaves, whisking well. Pass the mixture through a strainer and into a measuring jug. Pour the hot jelly into the hole in the centre of the pie to fill and allow to cool in the fridge for at least 1 hour before slicing.

SAUSAGE & LENTIL CASSEROLE

A comforting, warming and homely recipe, this is a perfect way to use up that pack of lentils in the back of the cupboard or some leftover veg. It became a lockdown staple for us, full of earthy flavours.

Serves 4

2 tablespoons vegetable oil
8 thick, good-quality sausages
chunky bread, to serve
dressed mixed green salad, to serve

For the lentils
2 tablespoons vegetable oil
2 onions, roughly diced
1 garlic clove, chopped
1 teaspoon hot smoked paprika
2 tablespoons tomato purée
500g tomato passata
500ml chicken or vegetable stock, plus an extra 500ml if needed
250g dried Puy lentils, washed and drained
1 tablespoon olive oil
salt and freshly ground pepper
½ bunch of basil leaves, torn, to garnish

Preheat the oven to 200°C/180°C fan/Gas mark 6.

First, prepare the lentils. Heat the vegetable oil in a large casserole dish over a medium heat. Add the onions and season well with salt and pepper. Cook for about 10 minutes until soft, then add the garlic and cook for another couple of minutes.

Stir in the smoked paprika followed by the tomato purée. Cook for another minute. Then, slowly add the liquids – the passata and stock. Season again with salt and pepper. Gently bring to the boil. Add the lentils and stir them into the tomato mixture. Cover with a lid or foil and place in the oven. Cook for 20 minutes, stirring halfway through. If the mixture becomes too dry and the lentils are not soft, add another 500ml of chicken stock and continue cooking until the lentils are soft.

Meanwhile, cook the sausages. Heat the vegetable oil in a large frying pan over a medium heat. Place the sausages in the pan, season well and fry until golden brown on the outside – they don't need to be fully cooked through at this stage.

Once the lentils are ready, remove them from the oven, stir and check the seasoning. Place the hot sausages on top of the soft lentils, pressing them down until they are slightly submerged. Drizzle the olive oil across the top. Put the lid back on and return the casserole to the oven for a final 10 minutes to allow the sausages to cook through.

Remove from the oven and garnish with torn basil leaves. Serve in bowls with chunky bread and a green salad dressed in a vinaigrette.

SINGAPORE NOODLES

Sautéeing the ham first gives this dish a meaty base, before you cook the remaining ingredients. I use dry-cured ham from the city of Jinhua in Zhejiang Province.

Serves 2

1 tablespoon vegetable oil
2 wafer-thin slices of Jinhua ham, thinly sliced
1 teaspoon spice mix (see below)
½ egg, lightly beaten
¼ red pepper, cored, deseeded and
    finely sliced
20g bean sprouts
¼ onion, finely sliced
green part of 1 spring onion, cut into
    2cm pieces
1 tablespoon diced Chinese fish
    cake (optional)
200g dried rice vermicelli noodles, rehydrated
    in boiling water, then drained and cooled
1 tablespoon diced Char Siu roasted pork
1 tablespoon fish sauce
1 tablespoon Shaoxing rice wine
1 teaspoon sesame oil
salt and white pepper

For the spice mix
1 teaspoon curry powder
1 teaspoon smoked paprika
1 teaspoon garam masala

First, make the spice mix simply by mixing the ingredients together. You'll need only 1 teaspoon of the mixture for the recipe, but store the remainder in a sealed container for other dishes.

Place a wok on a medium–high heat. When hot, add the vegetable oil, allow to heat up, then add the ham and lightly fry to infuse the oil. Add 1 teaspoon of the spice mix and lightly fry until fragrant.

Increase the heat slightly and add the beaten egg. When it begins to solidify, add all the prepared vegetables, followed by the fish cake, noodles and pork. Mix all the ingredients together in the wok until everything is well coated in the spice mix.

Add the fish sauce and rice wine and continue to cook for a few minutes. Finish by drizzling with the sesame oil and seasoning with salt and pepper. Serve immediately.

Chef's notes...

If you can't source Jinhua ham, then you can use Iberico ham instead, and honey roast ham can be substituted for the Char Siu roasted pork.

   The spice mix will keep for months in an airtight container if well sealed, and will be delicious added to a variety of dishes.

Stephen Terry

A KIND OF SPANISH TOAD IN THE HOLE

Quite often we have some batter left over from making the Yorkshire puddings on a Sunday at the Hardwick and I will occasionally take it home with me to make this dish on a Monday. So, it's a toad in the hole of sorts with a kind of Spanish twist, and I like to cook mine in a rustic earthenware ovenproof dish.

Of course, I've used ingredients that I love, but I believe a recipe should be inspiration, so feel free to swap in items you prefer or have to hand.

Serves 6 hungry people

olive oil
10 good-quality pork sausages
8 spicy cooking chorizo sausages
2 large red onions, peeled and each cut into
    about 12 wedges through the root
3 large Maris Piper potatoes, peeled, cut into
    about 4cm dice, boiled until just cooked,
    then cooled and chilled
3 garlic cloves, thinly sliced
200g manchego cheese, coarsely grated
6 eggs
crème fraîche, to serve (optional)

For the batter
5 eggs
250g plain flour
250g whole milk

Drizzle a little olive oil into a large non-stick frying pan over a medium–high heat. When hot, add the pork sausages and fry until light golden brown all over. Remove the sausages from the pan and put them into your chosen baking dish.

Add the chorizo sausages to the same pan and cook them on a low–medium heat for about 8 minutes. They will not colour too much, but will release their spicy red oil into the pan. Put these with the pork sausages.

Add red onion wedges to the same pan and fry over a medium heat so they start to caramelise in the olive and chorizo oils, which should take about 5 minutes. Use a slotted spoon to transfer the onions to the dish with the sausages, leaving the oil in the pan (drain it back in if you need to).

Repeat the process with the cooked, chilled potatoes, until they take on some colour. At the last minute, add the garlic slices and cook for 1 minute, until light brown. Add the potatoes and garlic to the dish with all the other ingredients, and use some of the oil from the pan to coat or brush the dish to ensure the batter doesn't stick.

Preheat the oven to 200°C/180°C fan/Gas mark 6. To make the batter, crack the 5 eggs into a jug and beat lightly. Put the flour in a bowl and make a well in the centre. Add the eggs and milk and thoroughly combine to form a batter. Pass this through a fine sieve to make sure it's smooth.

Place the baking dish in the oven for 5 minutes, then remove it from the oven and pour the batter over the sausages, onions and potatoes. Return it to the oven for 30 minutes, until the batter is risen and golden brown.

Remove the dish from the oven and sprinkle over the grated manchego. Then crack the eggs on to the surface and return the dish to the oven for 8–10 minutes, until the eggs are lightly cooked. Remove from the oven, portion and serve. I quite like a blob of nice, sour crème fraîche with mine. And a beer (preferably Spanish), of course!

Saiphin Moore

CHILLI, BASIL & MINCED PORK STIR FRY

Chilli and basil stir fry is also known as the 'lazy man' dish in Thailand as it's the dish you have when you can't think of anything else to eat. You don't need too many ingredients and it's quick to make. It's a proper comfort dish, full of chilli and garlic and served with steaming hot rice. Perfect lockdown food.

Serves 4

6 garlic cloves, peeled
4–6 red bird's-eye chillies, to taste
4 tablespoons vegetable oil
400g minced pork
2 tablespoons Thai fish sauce
2 tablespoons light soy sauce
1 tablespoon oyster sauce
1 tablespoon granulated sugar
100g green beans, trimmed and chopped
   into 5cm pieces
1 small onion, sliced
½ large red chilli, deseeded and
   sliced (optional)
4 kaffir lime leaves, chopped
large handful of Thai holy basil or Italian
   basil leaves
steamed jasmine rice and crispy fried egg,
   to serve

Using a pestle and mortar or food processor, crush the garlic and bird's-eye chillies together into a rough paste.

Heat the oil in a wok over a medium heat. When hot, add the chilli and garlic paste and stir fry for 1 minute.

Add the minced pork and stir in the fish sauce, light soy sauce, oyster sauce and sugar. Toss to mix well and stir fry until the meat is cooked through (about 3–4 minutes).

Add the green beans, onion and sliced red chilli (if using) and cook for 30 seconds–1 minute, until the beans have slightly softened. Turn off the heat, then add the lime leaves and basil and stir through.

Serve with jasmine rice and a crispy fried egg.

desserts & bakes

Claire Clark

GIN & TONIC JELLIES

These sublime jellies make the best after-dinner treats and will leave everyone in awe of your creative talents. Gin has become a very popular tipple – even the nation's firm favourite – in recent years. These little jewelled jellies are easy to make and hard to beat – they really pack in the flavour of gin. With more than 300 gin producers in the UK alone, there are plenty of gins to choose from – use your favourite.

Makes 16

6 silver or platinum-grade gelatine leaves
250ml tonic water
120g caster sugar
90ml your favourite gin

For the crystal coating
225g granulated sugar
finely grated zest of 1 lemon

Soak the gelatine leaves in a bowl of very cold water for a minute or so, until softened.

Meanwhile, heat 50ml of the tonic water in a pan with the caster sugar, stirring until the sugar has dissolved.

Remove the pan from the heat. Squeeze out the excess water from the gelatine leaves and add them to the pan, stirring well until the leaves dissolve. Add the rest of the tonic and then add the gin. Strain the mixture through a fine sieve into a 900g loaf tin. Place in the fridge for 4–6 hours, until set.

While the jelly is setting, make the crystal coating. Put 200g of the granulated sugar into a small bowl with the grated lemon zest and mix well.

Dust a chopping board with the remaining granulated sugar, then 15 minutes before you intend to serve, briefly dip the base of the loaf tin in hot water to loosen the jelly. Turn out the jelly on to the board. Using a sharp knife, cut the jelly into bite-sized pieces, then toss the cubes in the granulated sugar and lemon zest mixture. Serve immediately.

Chef's notes...

You can make the jelly in advance and keep it in the fridge for up to three days. Always roll it in the lemon sugar, though, just prior to serving, as this way the sugar will remain crunchy and add a jewel-like exterior, as well as a lovely texture to the jellies.

Heston Blumenthal

APPLE TARTE TATIN

This dish shows you that there is no right or wrong in cooking. Born out of a happy accident in the kitchen of the Tatin sisters over 100 years ago, it is one of my favourite desserts. If you buy ready-made puff pastry then there are only 4 key ingredients to it, so it allows you to connect with each and every one of them as they cook. You may only have a quartet of instruments but by being aware of all the interplay between the sugar, butter, apples and pastry you can still create a symphony!

I've cooked this perhaps more than any other dessert over the last year, and its warming, comforting flavours have reminded me that when so many of the things that we take for granted, like socialising and travel, have been taken away from us, there are still wonderful things we can experience at home in the kitchen.

The choice of apple is important as is the attention and awareness of the caramel as it slowly browns and intensifies in flavour. Although it's such a familiar dish, I always find something new and interesting in it each time I make it.

Serves 6

For the poached apples
600g apple juice
20g black tea leaves
500g unrefined caster sugar
250g unsalted butter, cubed
15g cardamom pods, crushed
4 cinnamon sticks
5g whole cloves
strips of zest from 2 lemons (use a vegetable peeler)
strips of zest from 1 orange (use a vegetable peeler)
40g runny honey
20g mint leaves
6 Granny Smith apples

To poach the apples, bring 500g of the apple juice to the boil, then remove it from the heat. Add the tea leaves and allow to brew for 3 minutes. Strain the juice, discarding the leaves. The apple juice may have evaporated a little when brought to the boil, so adjust it by topping up with the additional apple juice to yield 500g again.

Place the sugar in a deep saucepan over a medium heat and leave to dissolve to a dry caramel. Once the caramel darkens, add the butter, and mix to combine. Carefully add the apple juice to the caramel and stir thoroughly to ensure any hardened caramel melts.

In the meantime, in a separate hot pan, toast the crushed cardamom pods, cinnamon sticks and the cloves until fragrant. Add the apple caramel, citrus peels and runny honey. Reduce the heat to medium–low and bring to a gentle simmer for 20 minutes. Remove the pan from the heat, add the mint leaves and allow to cool to room temperature. Strain the mixture, discarding the spices, peelings and mint. Reserve the liquid.

Peel and core the apples. Place the liquid back into a pan over a medium heat. Add the apples to the liquid and poach until they are soft to the touch but still firm (about 10–15 minutes). Remove the pan from the heat and allow the apples to cool in the liquid completely. Remove the apples from the poaching liquid and place them upright on a board, discarding the liquid. Using a sharp knife, cut the apples in half widthways. Refrigerate until needed.

For the tarte Tatin, preheat the oven to 180°C/160°C fan/Gas mark 4.

Place the sugar into a straight-sided ovenproof frying pan (approximately 21cm in diameter) and place over a medium–low heat. Allow the sugar to begin caramelising, but do not stir until most of it has dissolved, then mix in any undissolved sugar with a spatula. Add the butter until well combined, then allow to cool slightly. Arrange the apple halves, cut-side up, around the pan, packing them as tightly as possible. Allow to stand for 5 minutes.

Roll the puff pastry into a circle between 2 sheets of baking paper to a thickness of 4mm and about 3cm

For the tarte Tatin
150g unrefined caster sugar
75g unsalted butter, diced
600g all-butter puff pastry
ground cinnamon, to taste
ground cardamom, to taste
vanilla ice cream, to serve

larger than the diameter of the pan. Roll the edge of the pastry about 2cm inwards to create a lip – this will give a nice crispy edge. Place the puff pastry, rolled-edge-side up, on top of the apples, making sure to tuck the pastry edges inside the pan. Bake for 30–35 minutes, or until the pastry is golden.

Remove the Tatin from the oven and allow to rest for 2–3 minutes – this will allow the caramel to thicken, making the Tatin easier to turn. Place a plate that is just larger than the diameter of the pan on top of the Tatin and turn the pan upside down, being careful of the hot caramel that may spill out.

Remove the pan and allow the Tatin to sit for 5 minutes. Sprinkle a little ground cinnamon and ground cardamom on top.

Serve the tarte Tatin with your favourite vanilla ice cream.

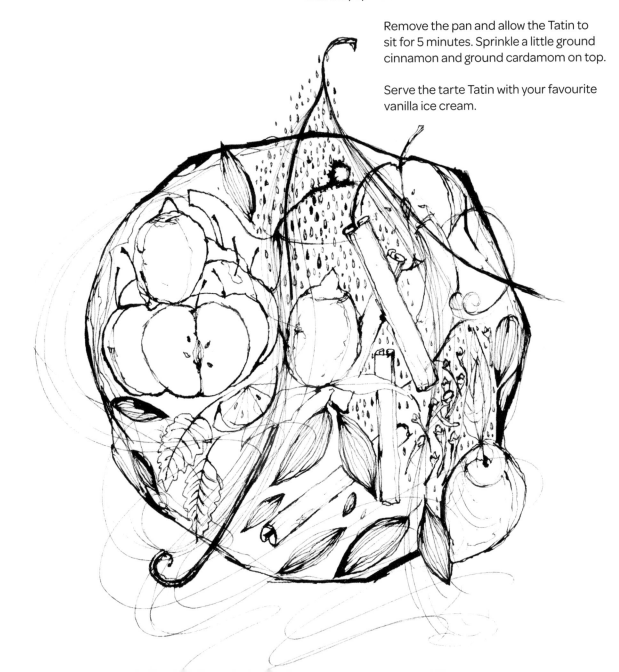

Nieves Barragán Mohacho

TORRIJAS
with orange sauce

*Usually you'd use old bread to make torrijas –
it's what people used to eat when their bread
went stale – but I like to use brioche, as it's more
buttery, and naughtier. You can make the orange
sauce in advance and keep it in the fridge for up
to a week. The dessert can be served hot or cold.*

Serves 4–6

250ml whole milk
250ml double cream
1 cinnamon stick
175g caster sugar, plus extra for sprinkling
juice of 1 lemon
250g brioche (about ½ a loaf)
knob of unsalted butter, to caramelise
    (25g-ish)

For the orange sauce
1 orange (preferably Seville)
40g caster sugar
50g Ponche Caballero or Cointreau
1 cinnamon stick

First, make the orange sauce. Peel the orange without
including any of the pith, then cut the peel into shreds.
Divide the orange into segments and remove the
membrane and any remaining pith.

Put the orange peel and segments into a pan on a
low–medium heat with the rest of the orange-sauce
ingredients and 20ml of water. Stir together gently.
Cook for about 15 minutes, stirring all the time – the
mixture will start to break down and become almost
like marmalade. Add a splash more water if it looks like
it needs it – it should be thick, not too runny. Set aside
while you make the torrijas.

Put the milk and cream in a pan with the cinnamon,
sugar and lemon juice. Heat gently to dissolve the sugar
and infuse the milk, then leave to cool.

Meanwhile, cut the crusts off the brioche (discard
the crusts), then cut the brioche into thick (3cm) slices.
Cut the slices in half to give 3 x 3cm chunks. Put the
bread into a container in a single layer and pour over
the infused milk. Cover with cling film and leave in the
fridge overnight.

The next day, the brioche should have soaked up all
the milk. Put the butter into a frying pan on a medium
heat. When it's melted, sprinkle over a little sugar, then
add the brioche pieces to the pan. Caramelise the
brioche pieces, turning until golden brown on all sides
and sprinkling with more sugar as you turn – they
should be crispy on the outside but milky within.

Spoon the orange sauce on to a plate and put
the torrijas on top – serve just as it is, or with vanilla
ice cream.

CHOCOLATE MOUSSE
with my favourite candy bars

This, folks, is exactly that! The recipe for this simple but amazingly delicious and unctuous (love that word!) mousse came from my butty (that's Welsh for mate) Tim Hughes, who is Chef Director of Caprice Holdings. I had dinner at Scott's years ago and begged him for the recipe, and I have used it ever since.

The candy bar part is quite subjective, as we all have our favourites. Personally, I'm going with a couple of classics: Maltesers and Mars Bar. I like to serve the mousse in glass dishes.

Serves 6

For the caramel sauce
100g caster sugar
10g salted butter
good pinch of sea salt
60ml double cream

For the mousse
3 regular-sized bags of Maltesers
100g good-quality milk chocolate,
    broken up
100g good-quality 70% dark chocolate,
    broken up
110g salted butter
8 egg yolks
4 egg whites
2 regular-sized Mars Bars, chilled, to serve

First, make the caramel sauce. Put the sugar in a small saucepan with 50ml of water and place over a medium heat. When the water has evaporated and the sugar begins to thicken and the colour is caramel (you can swirl the pan from time to time, but don't stir), take the pan off the heat and carefully add the butter, salt and cream. Stir altogether and set to one side.

Next, split the Maltesers equally (or not!) between the six glass dishes and set aside.

Now to make the mousse. Place both chocolates and the butter together into a heatproof bowl over a pan of simmering water and melt gently, stirring regularly. When the chocolates have completely melted, and are warmed and combined, remove the bowl from the heat and stir in the egg yolks thoroughly.

In a separate bowl, whisk the egg whites until stiff, then gently fold them into the chocolate mixture, ensuring that no white streaks remain.

Pour or spoon the mixture equally into your glass dishes and leave the mousses to set in the fridge for 2–3 hours.

To finish, dice up the chilled Mars Bars, then remove the mousses from the fridge. Divide the pieces of Mars equally on top of the mousses. Gently heat the salted caramel sauce and pour it over the top before serving.

fig 1.

Angela Hartnett

MUM'S BRAMLEY APPLE PIE

I grew up making this pie with my mum, who always used lard, and even after all these years I still seek her approval when I make this classic. Thank you for the recipe, mum!

I love the sharpness of the Bramley apples and the delicious pastry. It's perfect to eat warm or cold.

Serves 6–8

300g plain flour, plus extra for dusting
pinch of salt
75g lard, cubed
75g unsalted butter, cubed
ice-cold water
4 Bramley apples
100g golden demerara sugar, plus extra
    for sprinkling
whole milk, to glaze
double cream, to serve

Sift the flour and salt into a large mixing bowl. Add the lard and butter and use your fingertips to rub the fat through the flour to form a breadcrumb-like consistency.

Then, little by little, add ice-cold water and, using the blunt side of a knife, mix the flour and fat mixture until it forms a light ball.

Turn out the ball on to a lightly floured surface and gently knead. Cover with baking paper and leave to rest in the fridge while you prepare the apples.

Preheat the oven to 200°C/180°C fan/Gas mark 6.

Peel and core the apples and cut them into thin, even slices. Transfer them to a bowl, add the sugar and stir to coat. Leave to one side while you roll out the pastry.

Divide the pastry in half. On a lightly floured surface, roll out one half until it is nice and thin and large enough to cover the base and sides of a pie dish with a little overhang. Use the rolling pin to carefully transfer the pastry into the pie dish, gently pressing into the corners and edges.

Fill the pastry case with the apples so that they come up quite high.

Roll out the other pastry half and, again using the rolling pin, transfer the pastry to the pie dish and use it to cover the apples.

Use a fork to seal together the pastry lid and base around the edge of the pie dish, then use your knife to trim away the excess pastry. Use a pastry brush to lightly glaze the tart with the milk and sprinkle with a little sugar.

Place the pie on the middle shelf of the oven, and cook for 25 minutes, until golden brown. When it's ready, remove the pie from the oven and leave it to cool slightly before serving with double cream.

Simon Rimmer

VEGAN TOFFEE & BANANA PUDDING

Whilst many people turned their hand to banana bread during lockdown, I turned to this heart-warming pud. Sure to warm you up on a chilly night, my comforting toffee and banana pudding is laden with nostalgia alongside a modern vegan twist.

Serves 4–6

225g chopped dates
2 teaspoons bicarbonate of soda
110g vegan margarine spread
110g light brown soft sugar
200g self-raising flour
3 teaspoons ground ginger
2 teaspoons vanilla paste
2 teaspoons ground cinnamon
250ml almond milk
1 tablespoon golden syrup
1 tablespoon cider vinegar
2 overripe bananas, peeled and mashed
vegan vanilla ice cream or yoghurt, to serve

For the sauce
100g golden syrup
400g light brown soft sugar
300g vegan margarine spread
2 teaspoons vanilla paste

Preheat the oven to 180°C/160°C fan/Gas mark 4 and grease and line a 900g loaf tin.

Pour 200ml of water into a saucepan and add the dates and 1 teaspoon of the bicarbonate of soda. Bring to the boil and simmer for about 8 minutes, until soft. Set aside to cool.

In a mixing bowl, use a wooden spoon to beat the margarine and sugar together until soft and fluffy. Add the flour, ginger, vanilla, cinnamon and remaining teaspoon of bicarbonate of soda and gently fold together until no flour streaks remain. Add the almond milk, syrup, vinegar and bananas and stir to combine. Drain the chopped dates and stir them into the mix.

Spoon the batter into the prepared loaf tin and bake for about 45–50 minutes, until a skewer inserted into the centre comes out clean.

Meanwhile, prepare the sauce. Add all the ingredients to a saucepan and place over a medium heat. Simmer for 5 minutes, until the sugar has melted and the ingredients have combined.

When the pudding comes out of the oven, leave to cool slightly, then turn it out on to a serving dish. Pour over half the sauce, then serve in slices with vegan vanilla ice cream or vegan yoghurt, and the remaining sauce in a small jug for everyone to help themselves.

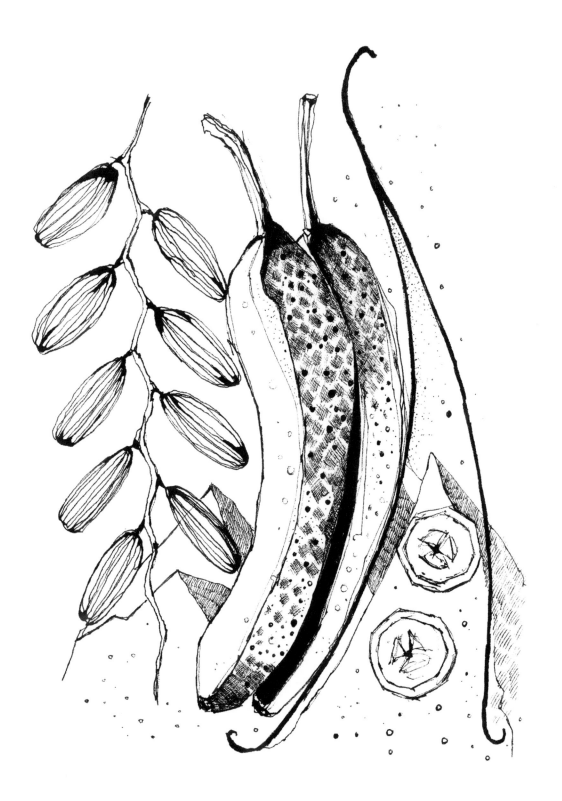

Nathan Outlaw

BAKED RICE PUDDING
with tropical fruit salsa

Who doesn't like creamy, comforting rice pudding? My version is really easy to make and uses coconut milk to add a little twist. The tropical fruit salsa is a lovely, refreshing addition that cuts through the creaminess and makes this dish a little more special. Make sure you choose fruit that is really ripe and ready-to-eat so that it's at its most flavoursome. We Outlaws love it!

Serves 4

For the baked rice pudding
500ml whole milk
250ml double cream
250ml coconut milk
½ teaspoon salt
2 lemongrass stalks
150g pudding rice
90g caster sugar

For the tropical fruit salsa
1 small ripe pineapple
4 ripe passionfruit
1 ripe mango

Preheat the oven to 160°C/140°C fan/Gas mark 3.

Put all the ingredients for the rice pudding into a large ovenproof pan and stir well. Bring to a simmer over a medium heat. Remove the pan from the heat. Cut a circle of baking paper large enough to cover the mixture and lay it on the surface. Transfer the pan to the oven and cook for 30 minutes, or until the rice is tender.

Meanwhile, prepare the salsa. Using a sharp knife, peel and core the pineapple. Cut the flesh into very small dice and place it in a bowl. Cut and scoop out the insides of the passionfruit, adding to the pineapple bowl. Peel the mango and cut into the same size dice as the pineapple. Add to the bowl and stir through thoroughly. Cover and keep cool, but do not refrigerate as this will suspend the flavours of the fruit.

When the rice pudding is ready, remove the lemongrass stalks and serve immediately, topped with the salsa.

Thuy Diem Pham

COCONUT & PEANUT BÁNH CAM

Super-tasty and really good fun to make with the kids, bánh cam are traditionally served with a mung-bean filling, but my current favourite is coconut and peanut, served with coconut cream custard. Delicious!

Makes 12 balls

250g white sesame seeds
1 litre vegetable oil

For the dough
225g glutinous rice flour
120g rice flour
50g potato flour
1 teaspoon baking powder
1 teaspoon olive oil
½ teaspoon salt
110g granulated sugar

For the filling
110g white granulated sugar
50g brown granulated sugar
150g coconut flesh
1 teaspoon vanilla extract
pinch of salt
100g crushed roasted peanuts
1 tablespoon tapioca starch

First, make the dough. Place all the flours, the baking powder and the oil into a large bowl. Mix together well and set aside for later.

Put 200ml of water, the salt and the sugar in a small saucepan over a medium heat and stir until the sugar has dissolved. Take the pan off the heat and allow to cool for 30 minutes, then add to the dough mixture.

Knead the dough until it is soft and smooth with no lumps, then set aside to rest for at least 3 hours. It will rise slightly and dry a little, which will make it easier to mould later.

Make the filling. Bring 150ml of water to the boil on a medium heat and add the white sugar. Leave until dissolved, then add the brown sugar and again wait until that has dissolved too. You will see that the liquid has started to caramelise and has a slight brown colour – at this point add the coconut flesh, vanilla extract and salt. Mix everything together well, turn the heat down to low and cook for a further 5–10 minutes.

Add the crushed peanuts and tapioca starch to the coconut mixture and stir until all the liquid has dissolved and the texture is thick and dense. You are aiming for the consistency to be dry and dense enough to be able to roll the filling into a ball while it still remains moist and pliable.

Turn off the heat, cool the filling to room temperature and then remove it from the pan and roll it into 12 even-sized balls. Set aside.

Now it's time for the fun part... Let's make some balls!

Split the dough mixture into 12 equal portions. Take the first portion, mould it into a thin disc on the palm of your hand and place one of your filling balls in the centre of the disc. Turn the edges in towards the centre and seal the dough, making it into as perfect a ball as you can. Avoid any gaps in the dough.

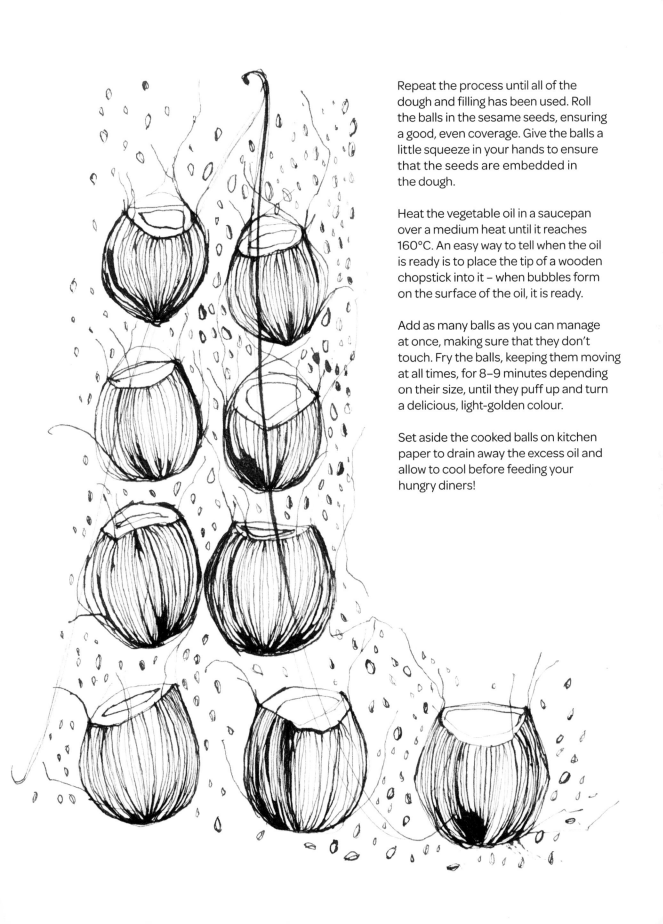

Repeat the process until all of the dough and filling has been used. Roll the balls in the sesame seeds, ensuring a good, even coverage. Give the balls a little squeeze in your hands to ensure that the seeds are embedded in the dough.

Heat the vegetable oil in a saucepan over a medium heat until it reaches 160°C. An easy way to tell when the oil is ready is to place the tip of a wooden chopstick into it – when bubbles form on the surface of the oil, it is ready.

Add as many balls as you can manage at once, making sure that they don't touch. Fry the balls, keeping them moving at all times, for 8–9 minutes depending on their size, until they puff up and turn a delicious, light-golden colour.

Set aside the cooked balls on kitchen paper to drain away the excess oil and allow to cool before feeding your hungry diners!

MERINGUES CHANTILLY
with strawberries & rosé

This is about as simple as a recipe gets – a handful of ingredients and a few lines of method. The reality is, however, that the success of the dish lies entirely in the quality of these ingredients and the execution of the recipe. Homogeneous, bright-white meringues topped with stiff whipped cream and poor, underripe, out-of-season strawberries will render a miserable affair. On the other hand, ivory-coloured meringues with crisp shells and chewy interiors, cloaked with a voluptuous whipped cream and topped with boozy, fragrant summer strawberries is an entirely different thing. Executed well, this is food fit for a king. The rosé provides a flavour that rang out through the summer months of our lockdown.

Serves 6

2 egg whites
145g caster sugar
300g strawberries, hulled, at
    room temperature
60g icing sugar
50ml Provençal rosé wine
150ml whipping cream
150ml double cream
pinch of salt

Preheat the oven to 150°C/130°C fan/Gas mark 2.

Place the egg whites in an electric stand mixer fitted with a whisk. Whisk the whites on low speed for 2 minutes or so, until they loosen up and become slightly aerated. Turn the speed up to medium and whisk for another 2 minutes, adding 120g of the sugar, 1 dessertspoonful at a time, then turn the speed up to high and whisk until the egg whites just start to form stiff peaks and you have a wonderful, rich and glossy meringue.

Line a baking tray with baking paper. Spoon the meringue into 6 large nests and place the tray into the oven. Immediately turn the oven down to 140°C/120°C fan/Gas mark 1 and cook the meringues for 1 hour, until they are crisp on the outside and still a little soft in the middle. Without opening the oven door, turn off the oven and leave the meringues to continue cooking as the oven cools – ideally overnight!

Meanwhile, prepare the strawberries. Quarter the strawberries and place them into a large mixing bowl. Dredge them with the icing sugar, toss them gently and set them aside to macerate for 1 hour, tossing from time to time. Add the rosé wine, stir gently and set aside.

Place the two creams into a bowl and add the remaining caster sugar and the salt. Whisk until the cream just forms soft peaks, but don't take it too far – it should still be loose enough to slump a bit when dolloped rather than a stiff mass.

To serve, place a meringue nest on to each plate. Dollop a generous spoonful of cream on to the meringue and finish with the strawberries and their sweetened, boozy juices.

Chris Galvin

CRÈME BRÛLÉE

A simple crème brûlée is one of life's greatest pleasures. It's very simple and perfect as it is, but when liberally sprinkled with caster sugar and blow-torched to form a caramel top, you get something truly delicious with a wonderful fragrance. You can easily flavour the brûlée with jasmine or raspberries, but in my opinion you can't beat the classic vanilla.

Serves 10

1.2 litres whole milk
seeds of 1 vanilla pod
6 eggs
3 egg yolks
175g caster sugar
boiling water from a kettle

For the glaze
200g caster sugar

Preheat the oven to 180°C/160°C fan/Gas mark 4.

Warm the milk and vanilla together in a pan over a low–medium heat until the mixture reaches a very gentle boil.

In a bowl, whisk the whole eggs, egg yolks and sugar together until very pale – almost white. Pour the hot vanilla milk into the egg and sugar mixture, whisking continuously until combined.

Pass the mixture through a sieve into ten 10cm ovenproof moulds. Place the filled moulds into a shallow baking tray and pour in the boiling water until it comes halfway up the sides of the moulds. Place the tray, with the moulds, in the oven for 30 minutes, until the mixture is soft set with a slight wobble. Remove from the oven and leave them to cool in the tray for 30 minutes, then remove from the tray and refrigerate for 4 hours to chill completely.

Just before serving, glaze the brûlées. Sprinkle equal amounts of the caster sugar on top of each portion, then use a kitchen blow torch to glaze to a golden colour. If you don't have a blow torch, you can place the brûlées under a very hot grill, carefully rotating to give an even colour. Allow to cool for 5 minutes for the topping to harden before serving.

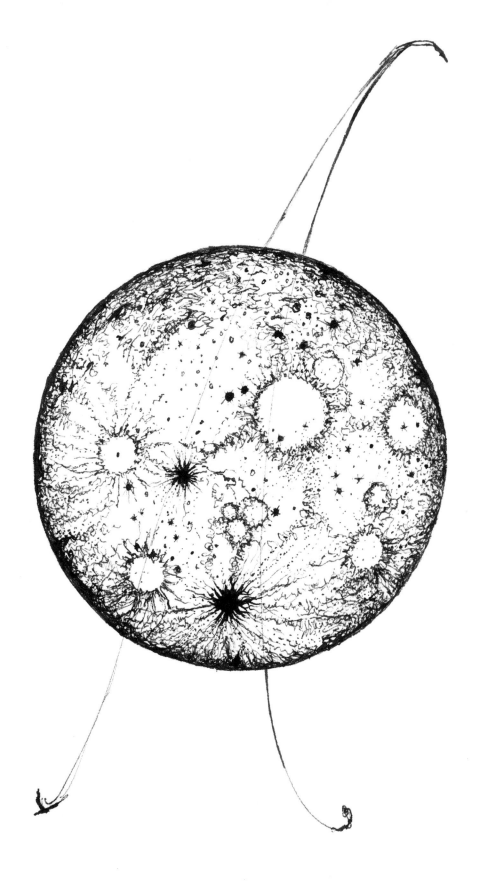

EGGLESS CHOCOLATE CAKE
the simplest method ever

There's no need for eggs in this incredible chocolate cake. Crisp on the outside and oozy on the inside, it's so easy and so delicious. I like to use hazelnuts, but almonds, pecans or cashews, or even a mixture, would be delicious. You could also try adding a sprinkling of dried fruit, such as a few sour cherries, raisins or apricots, to the mixture, or even chopped fudge or chocolate chips for extra indulgence. It'll make you happy for sure!

Serves 12

200g unsalted butter, softened, plus extra
   for greasing
200g hazelnuts
200g good-quality dark chocolate
200g self-raising flour
pinch of sea salt
200ml semi-skimmed milk
200g golden caster sugar

To serve (all optional)
good-quality dark chocolate, grated
fresh fruit and a dollop of yoghurt
scoops of vanilla ice cream
vanilla custard

Preheat the oven to 180°C/160°C fan/Gas mark 4. Grease and line a deep non-stick 25 x 25cm baking tin with greaseproof paper.

Blitz the nuts in a food processor until fine. With the processor still running, snap in the chocolate, then add the butter, followed by the flour and a pinch of sea salt. Pour in the milk, then add the sugar, letting the processor do all the work bringing it together. Once smooth and combined, use a spatula to help you tip the mixture into your lined tray, spreading it out in an even layer.

Bake for 18 minutes on the middle shelf of the oven, or until crispy and spongy at the edges, but still a bit gooey and wobbly in the middle. Now, you can either serve it warm with an extra grating of chocolate, some fresh fruit and a dollop of yoghurt, a scoop of ice cream or even a pouring of custard, and enjoy it like a pudding. Or, you can let it cool into more of a gooey brownie. Whatever you decide, enjoy!

Chef's notes...

For nutrition info, visit the recipe on jamieoliver.com

Gary Usher & Richard Sharples

CUSTARD TART

This tart is a staple on the menu at our third restaurant Hispi in Didsbury. We make one tart for each dinner service and once it's gone, it's gone. The recipe itself is based on that of a certain, famous steely-eyed chef, we've just tweaked our technique along the way and developed it into the version we like best. The addition of a little salt to the recipe really makes the custard come alive and it actually came about when chef Ryan accidentally spilt salt into our caster sugar bin and forgot to tell Kieran on the pastry section. A happy accident. Don't be too harsh on yourself if your custard is a little over set or your pastry a little soggy, it will always be delicious and you'll have an excuse to make it again.

The pastry and custard for this recipe are best made the day before you want to make the tart: this gives the pastry time to fully rest and it gives the ingredients for the custard time to become good friends. If you're a little short of time, make the pastry at least 4 hours before rolling your tart; the custard can be made just before use.

The tart is best eaten at room temperature. You can refrigerate it and eat it the next day; it's still delicious but a completely different thing.

Makes 1 tart

For the custard
250g egg yolks
800ml double cream
160g caster sugar
½ teaspoon fine salt

For the sweet pastry
350g plain flour
250g unsalted butter, cubed and chilled
125g caster sugar
1 egg, plus 1 egg yolk, beaten

To serve
1 nutmeg, grated

To make the pastry, place the flour, cubed-cold butter and sugar into the bowl of a stand mixer fitted with the beater attachment. Mix on a low speed until the butter has fully incorporated into the flour and sugar and has a consistency of breadcrumbs.

Meanwhile, crack the whole egg into a bowl and whisk until it is an even yellow colour. Add this to the flour mixture and work it on a low speed until a dough has just begun to form. The key word here is 'just'. Tip the dough out on to your work surface and use your hands to bring it together to form a ball. Wrap the dough tightly in cling film then push down on it slightly to form a round disc about 2cm thick. Place this in the fridge overnight or in the freezer for an hour if a little pressed for time.

To make the custard mix, gently combine all the ingredients together until the sugar is completely dissolved. Don't beat it as you need as little air in the custard as possible. Once the sugar is fully dissolved, pass the mixture through a fine sieve and refrigerate until you're ready to use it.

Once the pastry is fully chilled and well rested, remove it from the fridge, unwrap it and place on to a lightly floured work surface. Holding one end of your rolling pin, bash down on the dough, turning it 45 degrees each time you do, until you have a rough circle of around 18cm diameter. The reason for doing this is to work the pastry as little as possible and limit the amount of heat transfer from your hands to the rolling pin to the pastry. Now, using a more conventional method, roll the pastry into a circle around 24cm in diameter and 3mm thick. Gently roll the pastry up and around your rolling pin then lay it over a 20cm tart/sandwich tin. Gently press the pastry into all corners of the tin and leave all the excess hanging over the top. Check your pastry for any holes as this will be crucial to avoiding a soggy bottom, and nobody likes a soggy bottom. If you can see any holes, patch them up with any excess dough. Chill the pastry in its tin for at least 1 hour before starting to bake.

Preheat the oven to 180°C/160°C fan/Gas mark 4. Line the tart case with a piece of scrunched-up baking paper and fill it with baking beans or uncooked rice. Blind bake

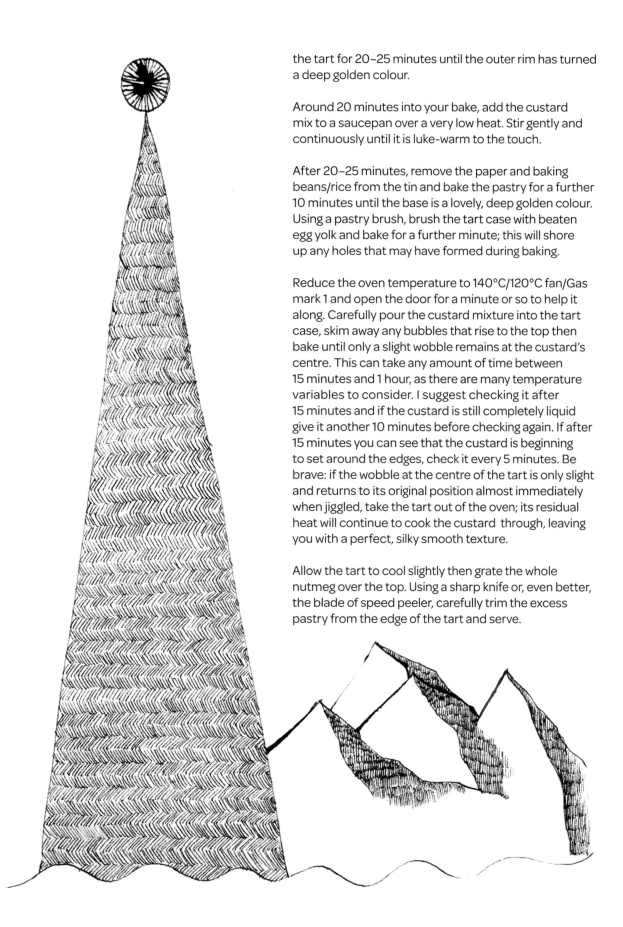

the tart for 20–25 minutes until the outer rim has turned a deep golden colour.

Around 20 minutes into your bake, add the custard mix to a saucepan over a very low heat. Stir gently and continuously until it is luke-warm to the touch.

After 20–25 minutes, remove the paper and baking beans/rice from the tin and bake the pastry for a further 10 minutes until the base is a lovely, deep golden colour. Using a pastry brush, brush the tart case with beaten egg yolk and bake for a further minute; this will shore up any holes that may have formed during baking.

Reduce the oven temperature to 140°C/120°C fan/Gas mark 1 and open the door for a minute or so to help it along. Carefully pour the custard mixture into the tart case, skim away any bubbles that rise to the top then bake until only a slight wobble remains at the custard's centre. This can take any amount of time between 15 minutes and 1 hour, as there are many temperature variables to consider. I suggest checking it after 15 minutes and if the custard is still completely liquid give it another 10 minutes before checking again. If after 15 minutes you can see that the custard is beginning to set around the edges, check it every 5 minutes. Be brave: if the wobble at the centre of the tart is only slight and returns to its original position almost immediately when jiggled, take the tart out of the oven; its residual heat will continue to cook the custard through, leaving you with a perfect, silky smooth texture.

Allow the tart to cool slightly then grate the whole nutmeg over the top. Using a sharp knife or, even better, the blade of speed peeler, carefully trim the excess pastry from the edge of the tart and serve.

Clare Smyth

WARM CHOCOLATE & LAVENDER TART

These tarts have finished every meal at Core since we opened three years ago. They were inspired by the chocolate tart at L'Ambroisie, the three-Michelin-starred restaurant in Paris. The tart itself is so simple – everything is in the execution. Serve them slightly soft in the middle, to be eaten just a few minutes after baking.

Makes 15

For the shortcrust pastry
188g unsalted butter
375g plain flour
1 teaspoon sea salt
3 large egg yolks (around 90g)
150g icing sugar

For the chocolate filling
125ml double cream
1 teaspoon dried lavender flowers
100g good-quality 70% dark chocolate, broken into small pieces (I use Udzungwa)
2 eggs
2 large egg yolks
50g caster sugar

Preheat the oven to 160°C/140°C fan/Gas mark 3. Make the pastry. Mix the butter, flour and salt together in a large mixing bowl to a crumbly texture.

Using a hand blender, in another bowl cream together the egg yolks and icing sugar until smooth. Add the wet ingredients to the dry ingredients and mix until everything comes together to form a dough.

Roll out the dough between two layers of baking paper until 5mm thick. Using a 6cm-diameter biscuit cutter, cut out 15 discs from the dough, re-rolling the trimmings as necessary. Then, using 30 round-shaped moulds each of 5 x 2cm, position 1 disc into 1 mould and press down with another (so that the dough is between the moulds). Repeat for all the discs. Trim any excess dough with a small knife.

Bake the tart cases for 6 minutes, until golden brown, then remove the top mould and set the cases aside to cool. Increase the oven temperature to 180°C/160°C fan/Gas mark 4.

Next, make the filling. In a small saucepan, heat the cream to 80°C on a cooking thermometer. Add the lavender and let it infuse for 4 minutes, then remove it from the heat and strain the cream through a sieve into a bowl. Add the chocolate, leave for a minute or so, then stir to melt the chocolate and create a ganache. Set aside at room temperature.

Using an electric hand whisk, in a large bowl mix the eggs, egg yolks and sugar until they are light and fluffy. Slowly pour and fold the ganache into the egg mixture using a spatula, until it forms a light brown mousse. Transfer the mousse into piping bags and set aside.

To assemble, snip the ends off the piping bags and pipe the chocolate mixture into the tart cases until it is level with each rim. Bake the tarts for about 6–8 minutes, until they are cooked with a very slight wobble in the middle. (If the filling is still too liquid, bake for a further 30 seconds.) Remove the tarts from the oven, leave to rest until cool enough to handle, then enjoy!

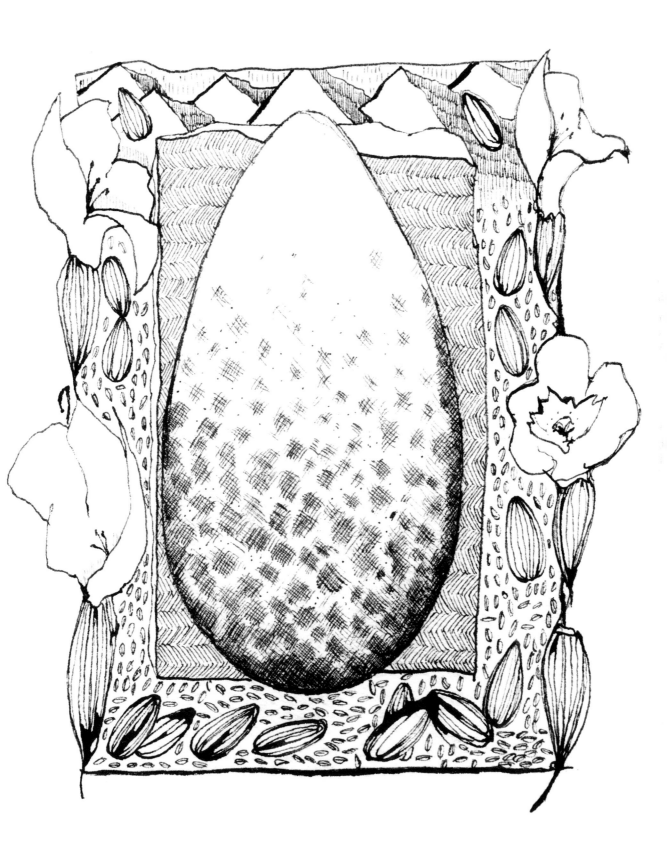

Tom Kerridge

QUICK BANANA ICE CREAM

An old-school family favourite of banana and custard – but not as you know it. This is a very quick dessert or sweet treat that can be whipped up as a little party trick. It also removes any need to fear making custard. Put your container and serving bowls into the freezer before you begin.

Serves 2

250ml ready-made custard
250g peeled, diced frozen banana
splash of whole milk
finely grated zest of 1 unwaxed lime
20g 70% dark chocolate, finely grated

This is as easy as it gets. Simply add the custard, frozen banana and splash of milk to a blender and purée to a smooth ice-cream consistency. Spoon the mixture into a pre-frozen container, then freeze for 10 minutes just to settle. Spoon the ice cream into frozen glasses or bowls.

To finish, sprinkle over the lime zest and grated chocolate and dig in straight away.

Ben Tish

WARM BLACK FIG & ALMOND PUDDINGS
with whipped mascarpone

Black figs come into their own in late summer and are with us through autumn – an absolute delight, reminding us of the sun-baked Mediterranean while we brace ourselves for a British winter. And that's where this recipe evolved – a Sicilian spin on a steamed British pudding. Choose really ripe figs that are almost bursting – the juices will ripple through the pudding adding sweetness and an appetising pink tinge to the almond sponge.

You'll need four 10cm heatproof pudding moulds for this recipe.

Serves 4

125g unsalted butter, softened, plus extra for greasing the moulds
90ml runny honey
5 black figs
125g caster sugar
2 eggs
70g plain flour
1 teaspoon baking powder
1 teaspoon ground cinnamon
100g ground almonds
30ml whole milk

To serve
150g mascarpone
50g icing sugar

Lightly grease the moulds with butter and divide the honey equally between them, allowing it to pool in the bottom of each mould.

Cut two figs in half widthways and place them cut-side down on top of the honey. Chop the rest of the figs into 1cm pieces.

Place the 125g of butter and the sugar in a stand mixer fitted with the beater attachment and cream together. One at time, add the eggs, beating well between each addition, until light and fluffy.

Sift the flour, baking powder, cinnamon and almonds into the creamed egg and sugar mixture, then fold it in. When incorporated, stir in the milk and the chopped figs. Divide the pudding mixture equally between the moulds, then place cling film over the tops followed by a layer of foil.

Place the moulds in a large saucepan and carefully pour water around them, so that it comes about two-thirds of the way up the sides of the moulds, then cover the pan with foil.

Place the pan over a medium heat, bring the water to the boil and steam the puddings for about 45 minutes, until risen and a skewer inserted into the centre of each pudding comes out clean (if the skewer isn't clean, return the puddings to the heat and check every 5 minutes or so, until done). Remove the puddings from the pan and leave to cool for 5 minutes.

While the puddings are cooling, whisk together the mascarpone and icing sugar.

Invert the puddings on to plates or bowls and serve with a dollop of the whipped mascarpone alongside.

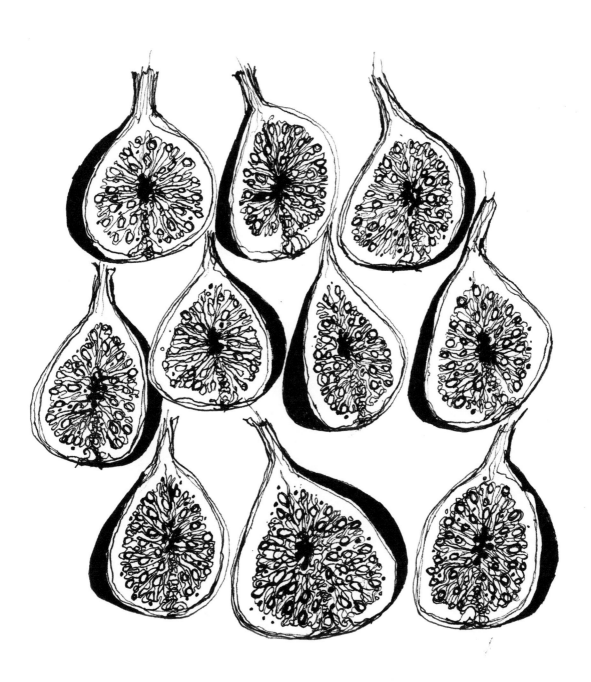

LIVERPOOL TART

I recently opened a restaurant in Liverpool, Lerpwl, and I wanted to include a recipe on the menu that celebrated the city. Some research found that there was a recipe for the Liverpool tart in a hand-written cookbook from 1897, and, with a little updating, it was ready for the new menu. It was originally called a Liverpool tart as the sugar and lemons used to come through Liverpool's docks, so all the ingredients would have come from the city.

This is a variation that is really easy to make at home, but just as delicious. If you have excess pastry you can freeze it for use another day.

Serves 8

For the sweet pastry
360g unsalted butter
225g icing sugar, sifted
6 egg yolks
75g ground almonds
610g plain flour, plus extra for dusting

For the filling
9 whole eggs
270ml double cream
150ml lemon juice
finely grated zest of 3 lemons
200g black treacle
370g dark brown soft sugar

Prepare the pastry. Cream together the butter and 150g of the icing sugar. Add the egg yolks and mix until combined.

Add the ground almonds, remaining 75g of icing sugar and 150g of the flour, and mix until combined.

Add the remaining flour and mix until a dough forms. Wrap the dough in cling film and leave to rest in the fridge for 1–2 hours.

Preheat the oven to 150°C/130°C fan/Gas mark 2.

Once the dough has rested, unwrap it and place it on a lightly floured surface. Roll it out to a disc 3–4mm thick, then use the pastry sheet to line a 20cm, loose-bottomed fluted tart case.

Line the inside of the tart case with greaseproof paper and fill with baking beans or uncooked rice and bake for 15 minutes. Remove the baking beans or rice and lightly brush the pastry with egg yolk. Bake for a further 10 minutes then remove from the oven and set aside while you make the filling.

Add all the filling ingredients to a heatproof mixing bowl and whisk them together until combined.

Place the bowl over a pan of simmering water and heat the mixture until it reaches 55°C on a cooking thermometer. Pour the filling into the tart case. Carefully transfer the tart to the oven and cook for 20 minutes, then lower the oven temperature to 140°C/120°C fan/Gas mark 1 and cook for a further 10 minutes, until the filling is firm at the edges with just a slight wobble at the centre (it will firm up as it cools).

Remove the tart from the oven and leave to set for up to 3 hours at room temperature before serving.

PARIS-BREST

Over 100 years ago Louis Durand, a French pastry chef, created a dessert to commemorate the Paris–Brest bicycle race. So as a keen cyclist what better dish was there for me to experiment with in lockdown? And if you're worried about the calories, just think of this as fuel before your next long bike ride!

Makes 6

For the choux pastry
pinch of salt
100g unsalted butter
200g plain flour
4 eggs
3 tablespoons flaked almonds

For the almond buttercream
8 egg yolks
250g caster sugar
250g unsalted butter, softened
35g almond paste

You will need
2 disposable piping bags
sugar thermometer

Preheat the oven to 160°C/140°C fan/Gas mark 2–3. Line a baking tray with baking paper.

Make the choux. Place 250ml of water, and the salt and butter in a large saucepan and bring to the boil. Remove from the heat and add the flour, then place the pan back on a medium heat and cook out for a few minutes to a smooth, thick dough.

Place the dough in a stand mixer fitted with the beater. Add the eggs one at a time, making sure each egg is fully combined before adding the next. The dough should look glossy and still retain its shape.

Transfer the dough to a piping bag, snip a 1cm hole in the end and pipe 6 rings on the lined baking tray, like a ring doughnut. Sprinkle over the flaked almonds. Bake the choux buns for about 20 minutes, until puffed up and golden. Remove from the oven and set aside on a wire rack to cool.

Meanwhile, prepare the almond buttercream. Whisk the egg yolks until light and creamy.

While the yolks are whisking, place the sugar in a small pan and add a touch of water, around 50ml. Place on a low–medium heat and allow the sugar to dissolve, then bring the mixture up to 121°C on a sugar thermometer.

Once the sugar is at 121°C, slowly pour it into the whipped egg yolks and gently stir as you go. Once fully combined, whip until cool, then add the butter, little by little, whisking all the while, until you have a nice creamy mixture.

Mix in the almond paste, then transfer the buttercream to a piping bag and set aside.

Once the choux buns are cool, split them in half, snip the end off the piping bag and pipe the buttercream on to each base. Place the lids on top and serve.

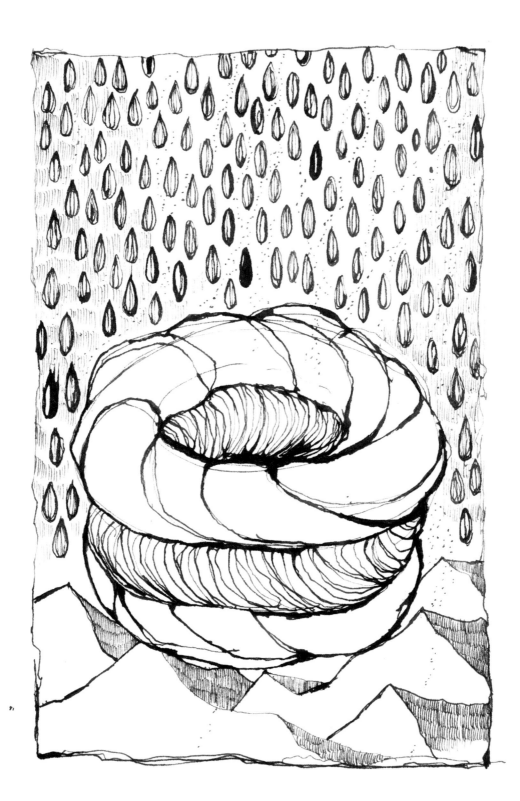

HOT PEARS
with blue cheese & walnuts

Pears, like apples, go well with lots of cheese because of their sweet and sour taste. You could eat this recipe as a cheese course, or double the quantities below and serve it as a starter.

Most crumbly blue cheese – stilton, cashel blue or even a roquefort – will work for this recipe. Or, it's a great way to use up the ends of a cheese board or whatever you may have left in the fridge.

Serves 2

2 ripe pears, Williams or Passe-Crassane
120g blue cheese, crumbled
60g walnuts, roughly chopped
1 tablespoon crème fraîche
1 tablespoon port
1 spring onion, sliced
salt and freshly ground black pepper

Preheat the oven to 180°C/160°C fan/Gas mark 4.

Cut the pears in half lengthways. Remove the seeds and core, then carefully scoop out some of the flesh without splitting the skin. This should leave you with 4 'boats'.

Roughly chop the pear flesh and add it to a bowl with the crumbled cheese and the walnuts. Fold in the crème fraîche, port, spring onion and seasoning.

Fill the 'boats' with equal amounts of the cheese mixture (you may have some mixture left over – refrigerate it to use as a topping for a salad), place them on a metal tray and bake them for 15 minutes, until browned.

MALT MERINGUES
with cocoa nibs & malt
chocolate ganache

These are a fabulous afternoon-tea delight – a sort of reinvented Malteser. And who doesn't love Maltesers? Invented in 1936, they were sold as a lighter option to other chocolate confectionery. My mum used to give us Horlicks to drink as children, before bedtime to aid restful sleep, and my love affair with malt started right there. It's such a fabulous flavour to combine with milk chocolate, as the buttery, milky flavours of the chocolate marry perfectly with the malt. The recipe might at first seem a little tricky: follow the method and you'll see it's actually quite simple.

Makes 8 tea-party-sized malt meringues

100g egg whites (about 3 large egg whites)
200g caster sugar
¼ teaspoon cream of tartar
15g cocoa powder
pinch of salt
30g malt powder, plus extra to decorate
30g icing sugar
25g cocoa nibs

For the ganache
200g milk chocolate, finely chopped
15g malt powder
100ml double cream

Preheat the oven to 105°C/85°C fan/Gas ½. Make sure all your utensils and the bowl are clean and free from grease, which can cause the meringue not to stiffen to firm peaks. Cut 2 pieces of baking paper to fit 2 baking sheets, ensuring each sheet of paper will lie flat. Before you line the trays, use a 5cm pastry cutter to draw 8 circles on each sheet of baking paper – leave a 2.5cm space between each. This is going to be your template for piping the malt meringues. Grease the baking tray and put the prepared baking paper pen-side downwards on to the tray. Fit a large piping bag with a plain 1cm piping nozzle.

Place the egg whites in the bowl of a stand mixer fitted with the whisk attachment. Add one third of the caster sugar and all the cream of tartar and whisk on a high speed until the eggs start to hold firm peaks. Add another third of the sugar and continue to whisk on a high speed for a further 2–3 minutes. The meringue should now look glossy. Add the remainder of the sugar and whisk on a medium speed for a further 3–4 minutes, until the meringue is thick and glossy.

Remove the bowl from the mixer. Sift together the cocoa powder, salt, malt powder and icing sugar into a separate bowl. Make sure you mix them well.

Using a large metal spoon, fold one third of the dry ingredients into the meringue. Do not do this with the machine as the fat from the malt powder will cause the meringues to go flat if the mixture is over-worked. Continue to fold in the dry ingredients, one third at a time, until they are all incorporated. Be as light and gentle as possible to keep as much volume as possible in the mixture.

Working quickly, fill the piping bag with the mixture and pipe 16 bulbs on to your prepared sheet of baking paper, using the circles as a guide. Speed is critical as the malt powder will start to break down the egg whites pretty quickly. Sprinkle the tops with the cocoa nibs.

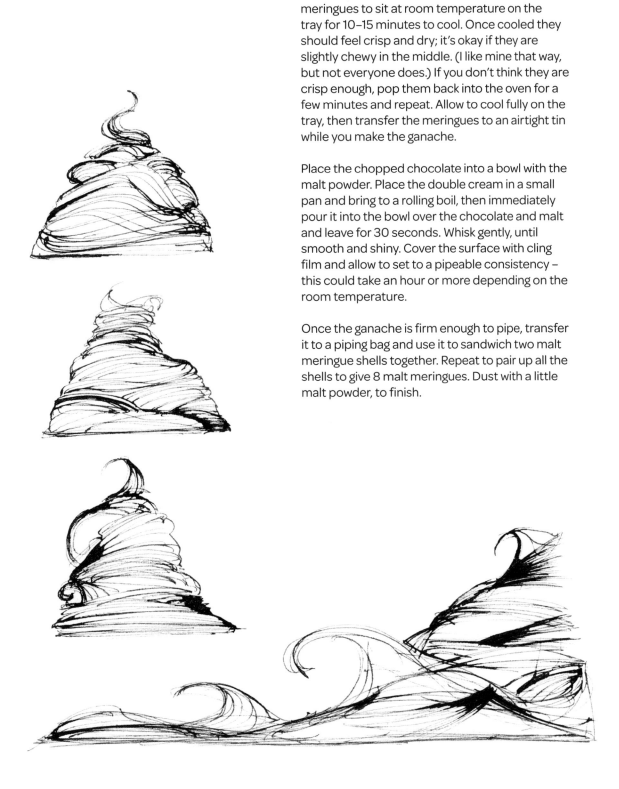

Bake immediately in the oven for about 1¾ hours, until crisp. To test for crispness, allow the baked meringues to sit at room temperature on the tray for 10–15 minutes to cool. Once cooled they should feel crisp and dry; it's okay if they are slightly chewy in the middle. (I like mine that way, but not everyone does.) If you don't think they are crisp enough, pop them back into the oven for a few minutes and repeat. Allow to cool fully on the tray, then transfer the meringues to an airtight tin while you make the ganache.

Place the chopped chocolate into a bowl with the malt powder. Place the double cream in a small pan and bring to a rolling boil, then immediately pour it into the bowl over the chocolate and malt and leave for 30 seconds. Whisk gently, until smooth and shiny. Cover the surface with cling film and allow to set to a pipeable consistency – this could take an hour or more depending on the room temperature.

Once the ganache is firm enough to pipe, transfer it to a piping bag and use it to sandwich two malt meringue shells together. Repeat to pair up all the shells to give 8 malt meringues. Dust with a little malt powder, to finish.

Nokx Majozi

MILK TART

The milk tart (or Melktert) is one of South Africa's traditional and most iconic desserts, and one of my favourites. With its baked crust, creamy milk custard and generous dusting of cinnamon, it is a taste of home.

Serves 6

400g digestive biscuits
1 teaspoon ground cinnamon
1 teaspoon ground nutmeg
110g unsalted butter, melted

For the filling
750ml whole milk
15g unsalted butter
1 x 390g tin of condensed milk
50g plain flour
50g cornflour
2 teaspoons vanilla essence
3 large eggs
2 teaspoons ground cinnamon

Preheat the oven to 180°C/160°C fan/Gas mark 4.

Blitz the biscuits to a fine crumb in a food processor. Add the cinnamon, nutmeg and melted butter and mix until well combined.

Place half the biscuit mixture in a 20cm springform tin, making sure it is distributed in an even layer and pressing down firmly with the back of a spoon.

Add the rest of the mixture to the tin, using it to create a 'wall' around the edge, pressing it firmly up the sides. Transfer the tin to the fridge for at least 30 minutes, to firm up. Remove the tin from the fridge, line it with baking parchment and fill with baking beans or uncooked rice. Transfer it to the oven to blind bake the biscuit casing for 10 minutes, until set and golden. Remove from the oven and leave to cool.

While the case is cooling, make the filling. Add 500ml of the milk, and the butter and condensed milk to a saucepan and place it over a medium heat. Stir, allowing the mixture to heat up until it reaches boiling point, then immediately remove it from the heat. Leave it to cool for about 20 minutes.

Place the flour, the cornflour, the remaining milk and the vanilla in a large bowl and whisk well to combine. Whisk in the eggs, one at a time.

Pour the egg mixture into the saucepan with the milk. Stir to combine, then return the pan to a low heat. Cook the filling, stirring continuously, for about 3–5 minutes, until you have a semi-thick, pourable custard. I use a thermometer when making custards; the mixture will start to thicken at around 70°C, but don't let it go above 80°C as otherwise it will scramble.

Pour the custard into the biscuit case in the tin and level it with a spoon. Dust with the cinnamon and leave the tart to cool at room temperature. Once cool, cover with foil and place the tart in the fridge for at least 6 hours to set. Remove the tart from the springform tin to serve.

Daniel Clifford

APPLE CRUMBLE
with cider vinegar pickled raisins & calvados custard

Is there a greater pudding than the humble apple crumble? The addition of the pickled white raisins adds a delicious extra dimension to the filling, and who can resist a homemade custard.

Serves 4

For the pickled white raisins
30g white raisins
100ml cider vinegar
100g caster sugar
100g apple juice

For the filling
100g caster sugar
50g unsalted butter
50g calvados
5 Braeburn apples, peeled, cored and cut into large slices
1 cinnamon stick
strip of lemon peel
pinch of salt

For the crumble topping
170g plain flour
110g golden caster sugar
110g unsalted butter, chilled
1 tablespoon rolled oats
1 tablespoon demerara sugar

For the custard
2 egg yolks
60g caster sugar
20g cornflour
450g whole milk
50ml calvados

Make the pickled raisins. Put all the ingredients in a small saucepan. Bring the liquid to the boil, then immediately remove the pan from the heat and allow the mixture to cool. Once thoroughly cooled, strain, discarding the liquid.

Preheat the oven to 190°C/170°C fan/Gas mark 5.

Make the filling. Place the sugar in a medium saucepan over a low heat until the sugar melts. Continue to cook for a few minutes, swirling the pan from time to time, but not stirring, until you have a golden caramel. Remove from the heat and add the butter, then return to the heat and add the calvados, taking care as it will spit.

Add the apples, cinnamon stick, lemon peel, pickled raisins and a pinch of salt. Place a lid on the pan and cook for 5 minutes, then remove the lid and reduce the liquor for about 10 minutes, until there's hardly any liquid left and the fruits are glazed. Remove the cinnamon stick and lemon peel and place the apple mixture into a baking dish that fits all the apples in a nice, deep layer.

Quickly prepare the crumble topping. Rub the flour, golden caster sugar and butter together in a bowl to form a crumble. Add the oats and pour the mixture on top of the apples. (The mixture may make more than you need – if so, you can freeze any extra for another time.) Sprinkle with the demerara sugar.

Bake the crumble for 30 minutes, or until golden brown on top.

While the crumble is cooking, prepare the custard. Whisk the yolks and sugar together, then add the cornflour and whisk again until smooth. Set aside.

In a pan, bring the milk to a simmer and pour it on to the egg yolks. Pour the mixture back into the pan and set it over a low heat. Stir until the custard coats the back of a spoon, then add the calvados. Serve warm with the crumble.

ESPRESSO PANNA COTTA

I'm not too good at desserts, but this is one I can make nice and easily. It looks great served in a small espresso cup, and it's all I need after a meal – a nice shot of coffee. I usually up the booze element for this one – here I've used brandy, but I'll often use whatever I have left in the spirits' cupboard. Everything works: Baileys can be quite nice, as can Tía Maria or Grand Marnier (that's when you are right at the back of the cupboard!).

Makes 12 espresso cups

220ml espresso or very, very strong coffee
220ml whole milk
120ml caster sugar
4 gelatine leaves
100ml brandy
360ml double cream

For the syrup
300ml caster sugar
125ml espresso or very, very strong coffee
25ml brandy

Heat the espresso, milk and sugar gently in a pan. Soften the gelatine leaves as per the packet instructions, then squeeze out the water and add them to the pan. Stir until completely dissolved. Remove the pan from the heat and stir in the brandy. Leave the mixture to cool.

Whisk the cream until it forms soft peaks, then gently fold it into the coffee mixture, trying not to knock out all the air. Divide the mixture equally into the espresso cups or moulds and transfer to the fridge for about 3 hours to chill until set.

Make the syrup. Warm the sugar in a saucepan on a low–medium heat, until dissolved, then let it bubble away until it has boiled down to a sticky caramel – take care that it doesn't burn. Stir in the coffee and the brandy and remove from the heat.

Serve the panna cotta with the syrup drizzled on the top (like the crema on an espresso).

John Williams

BAKEWELL TART

*My favourite recipes are the most simple
ones and my favourite flavour is anything that is
buttery. I love a buttery, fresh tart, filled with even
more buttery frangipane. I also like it with a strong
flavour of vanilla in the jam.*

Serves 6

For the sweet pastry
125g unsalted butter, cubed and chilled
95g caster sugar
1 large egg, lightly beaten
290g strong white bread flour, plus extra
    for blind baking
1 teaspoon fine salt

For the frangipane
125g unsalted butter, softened
125g caster sugar
2 large eggs, at room temperature
125g ground almonds
50g plain flour

For the filling
1 vanilla pod, seeds scraped or 1 teaspoon
    vanilla extract
5 tablespoons raspberry jam
40g flaked almonds

Make the pastry. In a bowl, combine the butter and sugar with a wooden spoon until soft. Gradually mix in the egg, then add the flour and salt in three batches, scraping down the sides of the bowl between each addition, until fully combined to form a dough. Press the dough into a thick disc shape, wrap it in cling film and refrigerate it for 2 hours, until thoroughly chilled.

While the pastry is chilling, make the frangipane. Beat together the butter and sugar in a stand mixer fitted with the beater attachment until light and fluffy. One at a time, add the eggs, scraping down the sides of the bowl and beating well between each addition, until everything is well mixed. Add the almonds and flour in three batches, mixing gently with a wooden spoon between each addition, until fully combined. Set aside until needed.

On a lightly floured work surface, roll out the chilled pastry until about 30cm in diameter and 3mm thick (about the thickness of a £1 coin), then use this to line a 22cm loose-bottomed tart tin. Leave to rest for another 45 minutes in the fridge.

Preheat the oven to 190°C/170°C fan/Gas mark 5.

Place four layers of heatproof cling film over the tart case and fill it with flour. Blind bake the tart case for about 20 minutes, until very light golden. Remove from the oven and discard the flour and cling film, then return the pastry case to the oven and bake for another 10 minutes, until golden.

Reduce the oven to 165°C/145°C fan/Gas mark 3.

Mix the vanilla seeds (or extract) with the jam then spoon into a disposable piping bag and snip the end to give a 1cm hole. Pipe the jam evenly over the tart base, then gently spread the frangipane over the top.

Sprinkle the top with flaked almonds and bake for about 30 minutes, or until golden on top.

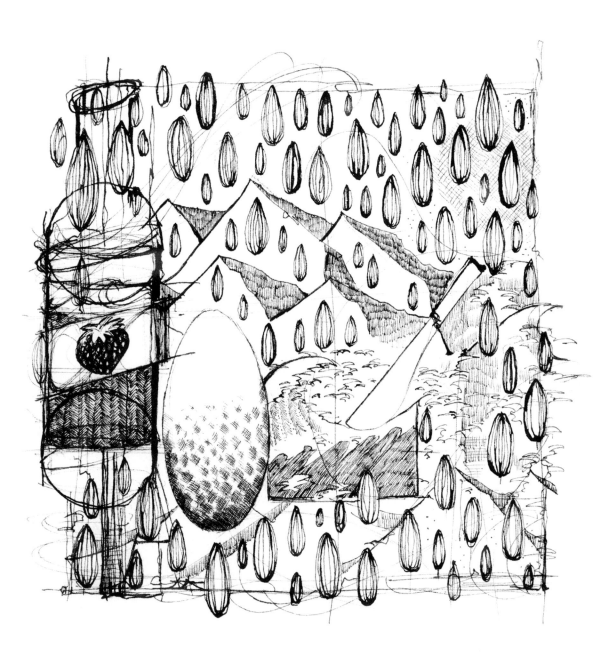

Giorgio Locatelli

LEMON & ALMOND POLENTA CAKE

Polenta is such a versatile ingredient and can be used in traditional Italian stews, pizza bases, chips, biscotti or, of course, cake. My lemon and almond polenta cake is distinctively Italian and so simple to make, why not give it a try?

Serves 8–10

230g unsalted butter, plus extra for greasing
60g whole almonds
230g light brown sugar, or demerara sugar
1 vanilla pod, seeds scraped
juice and finely grated zest of 4 unwaxed
    lemons, preferably Amalfi
4 eggs
230g ground almonds
175g polenta
2 teaspoons baking powder
150g caster sugar, for the glaze

Grease a 24cm round cake tin (about 8cm deep) with a little butter and line it with baking paper. Preheat the oven to 160°C/140°C fan/Gas mark 2–3.

Spread the almonds over a baking tray and bake for 8 minutes, shaking the tray from time to time so that the nuts are golden all over. Remove from the oven and leave to cool. Leave the oven on.

In a bowl, cream the butter, sugar, vanilla seeds and lemon zest until pale and fluffy. Fold in the eggs one at a time, making sure each is incorporated before adding the next.

In a separate bowl, mix together the ground almonds, polenta and baking powder, then fold this into the creamed mixture.

Finally, chop the roasted almonds and fold these into the cake batter. Leave the batter to rest for about 10 minutes, so that it absorbs all the ingredients and textures.

Spoon the batter into the cake tin and bake for 1 hour, until the cake is springy to the touch.

Just before you take the cake out of the oven, make a glaze. Whisk the caster sugar and lemon juice together until the sugar has dissolved.

When the cake is ready, remove it from the oven and put the tin on a wire rack. While the cake is still hot, spoon the glaze over the top. Leave the cake to cool, then remove it from the tin and serve.

Claude Bosi

BREAD &
BUTTER PUDDING

I can't resist a bread and butter pudding, it is the ultimate comfort food. This slightly decadent version of the classic dessert is one I often make at home, and it's well worth buying extra pastries so you have enough to make this with the leftovers.

Serves 6

15g dark raisins
50ml sherry vinegar
50g mixed pain au chocolate and croissants, cut into small pieces
15g chocolate pebbles

For the custard base
285ml double cream
140ml whole milk
3 vanilla pods
1 teaspoon vanilla extract
6 egg yolks
85g caster sugar

You'll need six 12cm-diameter ramekins for these individual puddings.

The day before you want to make the puddings, place the raisins in bowl, pour in the sherry vinegar, cover with cling film and leave overnight at room temperature.

When you're ready to bake, first make the custard base. Pour the cream and milk into a pan and add the vanilla pods and extract. Place over a medium–high heat and bring to the boil. Reduce the heat to very low and leave the milk to infuse for about 1 hour, then strain it through a sieve into a bowl and set to one side to cool. Discard the vanilla pods.

Once the milk mixture has cooled, in another bowl, cream together the egg yolks and the sugar, using a balloon whisk, until pale and creamy. Gradually whisk in the cooled milk mixture to combine. Reserve 200g of the custard in a separate bowl – you'll need this for the individual puddings; the rest will be served alongside.

Layer the pudding ingredients equally into each ramekin: start with some of the pastry pieces, then a scattering of soaked raisins (discard any residual soaking liquid), topped with some of the chocolate pieces. Finish with another layer of pastry pieces and the remaining chocolate pieces.

Divide the 200g of custard equally between the ramekins, pouring it over the layered ingredients. Allow the puddings to rest for at least 45 minutes so that the pastry pieces have soaked up the liquid.

Preheat the oven to 120°C/100°C fan/Gas mark ½–1.

Place the ramekins in a deep baking tin and fill the tin with boiling water to come halfway up the side of the ramekins, forming a bain-marie. Transfer to the oven and cook for 25 minutes, until the puddings are puffed up and golden.

Carefully lift the baking tray from the oven and remove the ramekins from the water. Set the puddings aside to cool a little, then serve warm with the remaining custard (reheated as necessary).

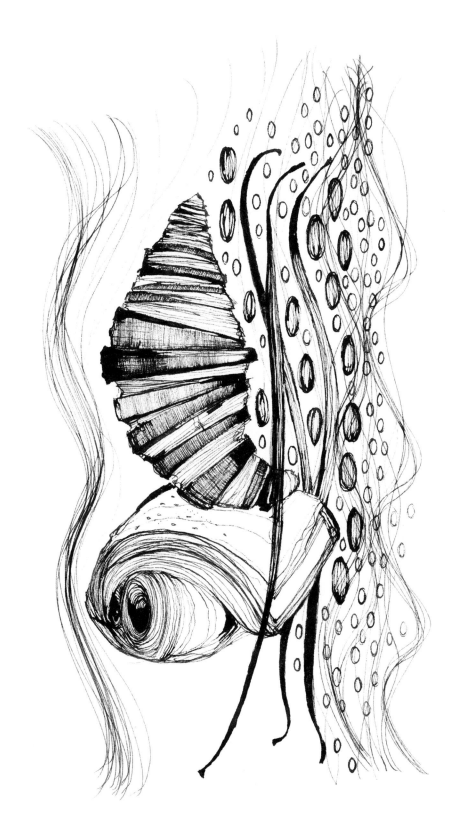

BANANA BREAD

Banana bread was one of the biggest hits on social media during the Covid lockdown (along with sourdoughs), and here's my version – with the addition of a homemade spice blend and the umami-rich white miso paste. I love this twist on the classic recipe with the savouriness of the miso; a bit like adding salt to caramel, but better! You can omit the miso, though, if it's just one ingredient too far.

The addition of coconut oil and light brown sugar will give you a softer and longer-lasting banana bread. If you can't source coconut oil, melted butter will work too.

Serves 8–10

125g melted coconut oil or unsalted butter, warm but not too hot
160g light brown soft sugar
4 ripe but not overly ripe bananas, 1 sliced, 3 left whole
2 large eggs
30g white miso
20g golden syrup
160g plain flour
1½ teaspoons baking powder
½ teaspoon bicarbonate of soda
1 teaspoon spice blend (see below), or to taste

For the spice blend
½ cinnamon stick
15 black peppercorns
½ teaspoon ground cardamom
½ teaspoon ground nutmeg

Using a pestle and mortar or a spice grinder, grind all the spice blend ingredients together to a powder and set aside.

Preheat the oven to 180°C/160°C fan/Gas mark 4 and line a 900g loaf tin with baking paper.

In a stand mixer fitted with the beater attachment, add the coconut oil or butter and the sugar and mix to combine.

In a separate bowl mash the 3 whole bananas with the eggs, miso and golden syrup.

Add the flour, baking powder, bicarbonate of soda and spice blend to the stand mixer and then add the banana mixture. Combine it all together, taste and adjust the spice if needed.

Pour the mixture into the loaf tin and transfer to the oven to bake for 20 minutes. Remove from the oven and top with the sliced banana, then bake again for a further 20–30 minutes. Use a skewer or cake tester to check that the loaf is cooked through and the middle isn't too wet.

Once baked, remove the banana bread from the oven and leave it in the loaf tin to cool for 5 minutes. Then, remove it from the tin and transfer it to a wire rack to cool completely.

BUTTERMILK & ELDERFLOWER PUDDING
with blueberries

This dessert is rather similar to an Italian panna cotta. In the UK we don't tend to use buttermilk that much, but in Ireland its use is fairly commonplace. You can get hold of it in good supermarkets and dairy shops, but if you're struggling to find it, just use Jersey milk instead. You can use different fruits as they come into season, or a mixture, or just one fruit as I have done here.

Serves 4

12g or 4 leaves of gelatine
350ml buttermilk
50g caster sugar
250ml double cream
100ml good-quality elderflower cordial

For the blueberry syrup
60g blueberries
2 tablespoons caster sugar

To serve
90g blueberries

Soak the gelatine in a bowl of cold water for a few minutes, until soft. Meanwhile, pour 100ml of the buttermilk into a small pan and add the sugar. Place over a medium heat, bring to the boil, then immediately remove from the heat. Squeeze out the gelatine leaves and add these to the pan with the hot milk. Stir until dissolved. Leave the mixture to cool.

Pour the cream and remaining buttermilk into a large jug. Whisk in the cooled buttermilk and gelatine mixture along with the elderflower cordial until combined.

Pour the mixture into 4 shallow moulds, or small pudding moulds or ramekins, then leave to set in the fridge for 2–3 hours, or overnight.

Meanwhile, make the syrup. Put the 60g of blueberries in a saucepan with the sugar on a low heat. Simmer for 2 minutes, or until the blueberries have softened. Strain the blueberry syrup through a sieve into a bowl, pushing the fruit through with the back of a spoon, then leave to cool.

To serve, dip the pudding moulds quickly in and out of hot water, then turn out the puddings on to individual serving plates. Scatter the blueberries around the puddings and spoon around the syrup.

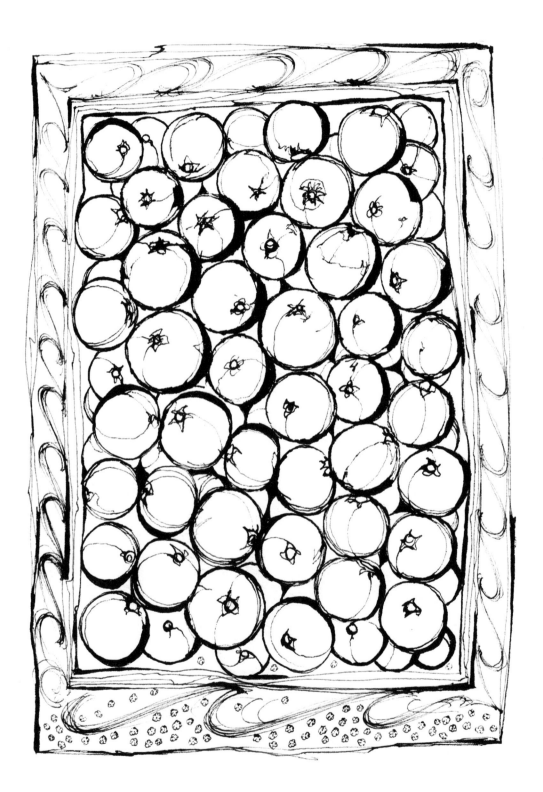

SPICED MIXED BERRY, WALNUT, RUM & PORT CAKE

In the 1970s I used to bake fruit cakes for weddings in India, and the method in this recipe – soaking the fruits for 2 days first – always made sure that the fruits remained suspended in the batter and did not settle down to the bottom of the cake.

Feel free to change up the dried fruits you use from my suggestions – all and any dried fruits will create a delicious cake. Here, I use cranberries, blueberries, golden raisins and some currants, which I keep in a large jar at home, forever soaking away. I put 200g of each dried fruit in the jar, cover them in port and dark rum and leave them for 2 days before using (after 8 hours is fine, but 2 days at least is better). The dried-fruit quantity here will yield more than you need for the cake. Once I remove what I need, I top up with some more fruit and more port, if need be, and leave them to soak for the next time.

Serves 10–12

For the berries
350ml port
150ml dark rum
500g sundried fruit (such as cranberries,
    blueberries, golden raisins and currants)

For the cake
100g walnuts
300g plain flour
1½ teaspoons baking powder
¼ teaspoon ground green cardamom
½ teaspoon ground cinnamon
½ teaspoon grated nutmeg
½ teaspoon salt
400g (soaked, drained weight) sundried fruit
250g unsalted butter, softened
200g caster sugar
6 eggs
½ teaspoon vanilla extract

A couple of days before you want to make the cake, combine the port and rum in a bowl and add the berries. Set aside and leave to marinate for 2 days.

On baking day, line a 23cm cake tin with baking paper and set aside. Preheat the oven to 120°C/100°C fan/Gas mark ½. Spread the walnuts on a baking tray and toast them in the oven for 20 minutes, until coloured. Remove from the oven, leave to cool, then coarsely chop.

Increase the oven temperature to 150°C/130°C fan/Gas mark 2.

Sift the flour, baking powder, cardamom, cinnamon, nutmeg and salt together into a large mixing bowl. Stir through the drained berries and chopped toasted walnuts to distribute evenly and set aside.

Beat the butter in a bowl with an electric hand beater or a wooden spoon until smooth and light. Gradually beat in the caster sugar until thoroughly incorporated. One at a time, add the eggs to the creamed butter and sugar mixture, beating well between each addition. Do remember that the mixture may look split but don't worry!

Fold in the sifted flour mixture, a little at a time, and blend it all together, taking care not to leave any lumps. Do not over beat, as you don't want the cake to sink. Add the vanilla.

Pour the mixture into the prepared cake tin and place it on the middle shelf of the oven. Bake for 1 hour, give or take, until a skewer or thin knife inserted into the centre of the cake comes out clean. As all ovens behave differently, the skewer check is the best way to tell whether or not your cake is done.

Remove the cake from the oven and transfer to a wire rack to cool. Slice and serve only when cold – even if the urge to succumb to the aromas feels overwhelming, resist! The cake is delicious with custard, cream or ice cream, or on its own with a cup of tea.

Contributors

PAUL AINSWORTH

With parents who ran a guest-house, hospitality runs in Paul's blood. After studying catering and hospitality at Southampton College, Paul went on to work with Gary Rhodes, Gordon Ramsay and Marcus Wareing, before moving to Padstow in Cornwall and working with his wife, Emma, to launch Paul Ainsworth at No.6, and going on to open other sites in Padstow and Rock.

- *The Croque Madame (see page 42)*
- *Cornish Cod Piperade with Cornish Mussels & Basil Mayonnaise (see page 124)*

JASON ATHERTON

Having worked alongside chefs including Pierre Koffmann, Marco Pierre White and Gordon Ramsay, Jason launched Pollen Street Social in 2011. The Social Company has grown since then, with a large and growing portfolio of restaurants worldwide. He is the Principal Patron of Hospitality Action.

- *Keziah's Ratatouille (see page 84)*
- *Spanish Chicken Casserole (see page 140)*

SAT BAINS

Having been inspired by Nottingham chef Mick Walton and reading Marco Pierre White's *White Heat*, Sat set out to be the best chef he could, moving to Oxford to work with Raymond Blanc and then on to London. In 1999 Sat won the Roux Scholarship. Eventually returning to Nottingham, in 2002 he opened Restaurant Sat Bains with Rooms.

- *Power Omelette (see page 28)*
- *Salmon en Papillote (see page 128)*

TOMMY BANKS

A proud Yorkshireman, Tommy serves up the county on a plate at The Black Swan, his family's pub, and his York-based restaurant Roots. Utilising produce from the family farm and foraged ingredients from the local area is at the cornerstone of his cooking.

- *Chorizo & Mozzarella Shakshuka (see page 16)*
- *Beer-braised Brisket Mac 'n Cheese (see page 168)*

NIEVES BARRAGÁN MOHACHO

Having grown up in Bilbao, Nieves was immersed in Basque produce and cuisine from an early age. She moved to London in 1998 and went on to become the Executive Chef for Harts Restaurant Group, launching the incredibly successful Barrafina. In 2018 Nieves opened Sabor, a food journey through Spain.

- *Grilled Courgettes with Parsnip Purée & Rocket Pesto (see page 74)*
- *Torrijas with Orange Sauce (see page 190)*

ELLIS BARRIE

One of the infamous Barrie Bros, Ellis attended a Saturday cooking course from the age of 12, and the rest is history. After his dad bought a campsite in Anglesey, Ellis and the family moved from Liverpool and threw themselves into making it a success. The campsite's shed turned restaurant, The Marram Grass, seeks to use the best of Welsh produce.

- *Barrie Baked Beans with Treacle Bread (see page 18)*
- *Liverpool Tart (see page 216)*

RAYMOND BLANC

Raymond grew up in rural France, helping his father grow vegetables to feed the family. First employed as a restaurant cleaner, he was soon promoted to pot wash and then waiter, before moving to England where he opened a restaurant in Oxford. In 1983 he spotted a country manor for sale and knew it would be the fulfilment of his dreams – and so Le Manoir aux Quat'Saisons was born.

- *Asparagus & Poached Eggs with Mustard Dressing (see page 68)*
- *Fillet of Mackerel with Shaved Fennel Salad & Soy Lime Glaze (see page 132)*

HESTON BLUMENTHAL

Although self-taught, Heston Blumenthal has pushed the boundaries of a traditional kitchen and changed the way people cook. Through his dedication to creativity and science, and his research into the history of British gastronomy, he has pioneered new techniques. He opened the internationally renowned The Fat Duck in 1995 and The Hinds Head in 2004, both in Bray. In 2011 Heston launched Dinner by

Heston Blumenthal in London and in 2014 The Perfectionists' Café inside Heathrow Airport.

- *Ratatouille (see page 102)*
- *Apple Tarte Tatin (see page 188)*

CLAUDE BOSI

Growing up in Lyon, Claude's parents ran a bistro, giving him his first taste of cooking, and at 14 he took up a place at catering college. He worked in some of France's best restaurants before moving to the UK in 1998. In 2000 Claude opened Hibiscus, which moved to London in 2007. In 2016, Claude closed Hibiscus and took over the reins at legendary London restaurant Bibendum.

- *Cornish Crab Quiche (see page 76)*
- *Bread & Butter Pudding (see page 234)*

TOM BROWN

Originally from Cornwall, Tom worked in restaurants across the south-west before he went to work for Nathan Outlaw, staying for a number of years. He was Head Chef at Nathan's restaurant at The Capital hotel in London, and in 2018 Tom opened his debut restaurant, Cornerstone. Since the launch, it has gone on to win many awards thanks to their dedication to British seafood and a world-class team which includes head chef, James Toth.

- *Crab Crumpet with Cauliflower & Parmesan (see page 40)*
- *Hake Kievs with Mushroom Butter & Hollandaise (see page 130)*

MICHAEL CAINES

Michael has built his reputation on a personal and distinctive modern cuisine, celebrating local and seasonal produce from Devon and the south-west, but drawing on influences from his travels around the world. In 2017 Michael opened Lympstone Manor Hotel, a luxury country house hotel overlooking the Exe estuary. The Michael Caines collection also comprises the Harbourside Refuge in Porthleven, The Cove at Maenporth and new for 2021 Mickeys Beach Bar and Restaurant in Exmouth.

- *Pumpkin Soup (see page 54)*
- *Lamb Koftas with Tzatziki (see page 156)*

CLAIRE CLARK

One of the world's best pastry chefs, Claire learnt her craft under legendary pâtissiers Ernst Bachmann and John Huber, before working in some of London's most prestigious restaurants, including Claridge's and The Wolseley. In 2005 she moved to California to take up the position of Head Pastry Chef at The French Laundry. Returning to the UK, Claire set up the Claire Clark Academy at Milton Keynes College and acts as a consultant to many of the UK's leading chefs.

- *Gin & Tonic Jellies (see page 186)*
- *Malt Meringues with Cocoa Nibs & Malt Chocolate Ganache (see page 222)*

DANIEL CLIFFORD

It was work experience in the kitchens at Canterbury University that changed Daniel's life, and set him on the path to being a chef. Renowned for his modern British cooking, with an unmistakeably French style, Daniel is the Chef Patron of Midsummer House in Cambridge.

- *Steak & Chips with Béarnaise Sauce (see page 166)*
- *Apple Crumble with Cider Vinegar Pickled Raisins & Calvados Custard (see page 226)*

JAMES COCHRAN

With roots in St Vincent in the Caribbean and Glasgow, Scotland, James grew up in Whitstable, Kent, where his love of seafood was kickstarted. He always wanted to be a chef, and moved to London to work at The Ledbury and The Harwood Arms, before taking the helm of his own restaurant 1251.

- *Buttermilk Chicken Wings (see page 90)*
- *Celeriac Tagliatelle with Seaweed, Cornish Cured Mackerel & 'Nduja (see page 112)*

RICHARD CORRIGAN

Richard has cooked all his life, opening numerous restaurants, as well as taking over the legendary Bentley's Oyster Bar and Grill – he also owns Corrigan's Mayfair, Daffodil Mulligan and Virginia Park Lodge in London, and he has cooked for the Queen. His passion for seasonal food is only matched by his enthusiasm for the ingredients to be found in Britain and Ireland.

- *Shellfish Cocktail (see page 78)*
- *Bentley's Fish Pie (see page 126)*

THUY DIEM PHAM

Having been born in Vietnam, Thuy moved with her family to the UK as a child. It is the memories of her childhood in south Vietnam, surrounded by an array of fresh produce, that is the foundation of her culinary creations. She is the owner and chef of The Little Viet Kitchen in Islington, London.

- *Lemongrass Chicken Bánh Mì (see page 36)*
- *Coconut & Peanut Bánh Cam (see page 200)*

CALUM FRANKLIN

Drawing on a wealth of culinary experience and a fascination with architecture, Calum is the Executive Chef of Holborn Dining Room, a grand British brasserie in the heart of London. He created The Pie Room in 2018, a kitchen and pie shop designed to reflect the nation's rich history of savoury pastry.

- *Pork & Black Pudding Piesolation (see page 172)*

CHRIS GALVIN

It was a need to support his family that led Chris to approach The Old Log looking for work, and it was there he discovered a passion for food. It was the start of a 30-year career that saw him work in some of the finest restaurants and hotels around the world, as well as opening a number of celebrated restaurants with his brother Jeff and launching Galvin's Chance, an into-work programme for young people.

- *Galvin Brothers' Burger (see page 158)*
- *Crème Brûlée (see page 204)*

ROBIN GILL

Leaving Dublin and moving to London to further his career, Robin landed a job at Marco Pierre White's restaurant The Oak Room. From there he moved to Italy, working at Don Alfonso, where

the focus was on seasonality and the importance of the produce. Returning to the UK, Robin initially worked a stage at Le Manoir aux Quat'Saisons, then staying on for many years before establishing The Dairy and other restaurants in London, with his wife Sarah.

- *My Irish Onion Soup (see page 52)*
- *Pasta Nerano (see page 108)*

LISA GOODWIN-ALLEN

With her culinary career starting at college, Lisa graduated and worked in several prestigious restaurants before joining Northcote aged just 20, becoming Executive Chef in 2015. At Northcote she has honed her passion for local suppliers and seasonal ingredients, as well as incorporating her Lancashire roots into her dishes.

- *Good Old Sausage Roll (see page 32)*
- *Spicy Lamb Meatballs with Three-cabbage Slaw & Yoghurt Pittas (see page 146)*

ELIZABETH HAIGH

Born in Singapore, Elizabeth moved to England at an early age. Returning to Singapore on family holidays she would soak up all its food and culinary traditions. She competed on *MasterChef*, and worked in various acclaimed restaurants before heading up the team at Pidgin. In 2019 she opened Mei Mei, a traditional *kopitiam* (Singaporean coffee shop) in Borough Market.

- *Fried Egg & Sambal with Rice & Soy Sauce (see page 88)*
- *Lamb Pastini with Parmesan Salad (see page 150)*

ANGELA HARTNETT

Born in Britain, Angela's passion for good, honest food and the best ingredients was instilled in her by her Italian grandmother and mother. She worked for Gordon Ramsay, opening a number of restaurants with him before opening Murano, where she is Chef Proprietor, as well as Café Murano and Hartnett Holder & Co at Lime Wood.

- *Bacon & Fried Egg Bun (see page 22)*
- *Mum's Bramley Apple Pie (see page 194)*

ANNA HAUGH

From Dublin, Anna has been cooking for almost 20 years, working in some of the world's best kitchens, including The Square, Pied a Terre and Paris' Hotel Lotti. She opened Myrtle restaurant in Chelsea in 2019, with cousin Daniel Haugh as front of house. At Myrtle, Anna serves food that celebrates her Irish heritage, classic French training and modern European influences.

- *Mushrooms on Toast with Boiled Eggs (see page 12)*
- *Black Pudding Burger with Cumin & Chilli Wedges (see page 170)*

MARK HIX

Having grown up in West Bay, Bridport, Mark took up a position at The Hilton, followed by Grosvenor House Hotel and then The Dorchester. He was the Executive Head Chef with Caprice Holdings, overseeing Le Caprice and The Ivy, for 18 years, before opening his own restaurants across the UK. In 2020, Mark opened HIX Oyster & Fish House in Lyme Regis, and invested in a fish truck selling the morning's catch.

- *Cuttlefish Ink Spelt (see page 116)*
- *Buttermilk & Elderflower Pudding with Blueberries (see page 238)*

PHIL HOWARD

Phil's career started at Roux Restaurants in 1988, before moving on to train under Marco Pierre White and then Simon Hopkinson. In 1991 he opened The Square, where he remained for 25 years. In 2016 Phil opened Elystan Street, where the focus is on vitality and flavour.

- *Chargrilled Beef Rump with a Feast of Onions, Field Mushrooms, Garlic & Potatoes (see page 160)*
- *Meringues Chantilly with Strawberries & Rosé (see page 202)*

NIALL KEATING

Having previously worked at some of the finest restaurants around the world, including Benu, Sat Bains and Kong Hans Kaelder, influencing his Asian-inspired dishes, Niall joined Whatley Manor as the Executive Chef in 2017. In 2018, aged just 26, he was named Michelin Young European Chef of the Year.

- *French Dip Sandwiches (see page 38)*
- *Paris-Brest (see page 218)*

TOM KERRIDGE

Born and raised in Gloucestershire, Tom dabbled in acting but ultimately fell in love with hospitality while at culinary school in Cheltenham. He worked in country house hotels and then moved to London to work with Gary Rhodes, among others. In 2005 Tom and wife Beth opened The Hand and Flowers. They have since gone on to open further restaurants and pubs in London, Manchester and Marlow.

- *Fish Finger Sandwich with Curried Mushy Peas (see page 44)*
- *Quick Banana Ice Cream (see page 212)*

SELIN KIAZIM

Having developed a love of food from a young age, Selin gained a distinction for her Professional Chef's Diploma and went on to work with acclaimed chef Peter Gordon. In 2015 Selin opened Oklava in London, with menus inspired by her Turkish Cypriot heritage, focused on communal eating and sharing dishes.

- *Halloumi Loaf (see page 46)*
- *Four Cheese, Garlic & Spring Onion Pide (see page 94)*

KRIS KIRKHAM

After spending 15 years training and working as a chef, Kris stepped out of the kitchen and moved into food and still life photography. His experiences as a chef fuel his passion for food and this is evident in his award-winning photography, which feature in this book's pages.

TOM KITCHIN

With early training at the Gleneagles Hotel, Tom has worked with some of the world's most renowned chefs, including Pierre Koffmann and Alain Ducasse. He opened The Kitchin with his wife, Michaela, in 2006 where he combined his first-class training with his passion for innovative seasonal cooking. They have since opened The Scran & Scallie and The Bonnie Badger.

- *Kedgeree (see page 24)*
- *Smoked Salmon & Spinach Lasagne (see page 120)*

ATUL KOCHHAR

Born in Jamshedpur in East India, Atul moved to the UK in 1994, quickly gaining acclaim in the industry. Atul's food is a melting pot of traditional techniques, combining the best spices and ingredients from India with the very best British ingredients. Atul has a growing restaurant portfolio, with Kanishka in Mayfair and sites in Marlow including Sindhu and Vaasu.

- *Jamshedpur-style Egg Rolls (see page 30)*
- *Mrs K's Chickpea Curry (see page 98)*

GIORGIO LOCATELLI

While he was growing up, Giorgio's uncle ran a restaurant, which gave him an appreciation of food from a young age. He worked in restaurants in Italy, Switzerland and Paris, before settling permanently in England. In 2002 Giorgio and his wife, Plaxy, opened their first independent restaurant, Locanda Locatelli, serving traditional Italian food.

- *Pan-fried Cauliflower Salad (see page 62)*
- *Lemon & Almond Polenta Cake (see page 232)*

DAVID LOFTUS

A celebrated, award-winning photographer, David is also a highly accomplished illustrator and contributed all the illustrations for this book. His photography has brought food to life for millions of people, featuring in some of our best-loved cookbooks.

NOKX MAJOZI

Originally from South Africa and having studied at Durban University of Technology, Nokx's first culinary role was at Durban's 4-star Riverside Hotel. She moved to London in 2002, and, after working at The Intercontinental Park Lane, The Landmark and Brown's, Nokx landed at Rosewood London and the Holborn Dining Room, where she is Sous Chef and Senior Pie Maker.

- *Lamb Bunny Chow (see page 152)*
- *Milk Tart (see page 224)*

JAMES MARTIN

North Yorkshire born and bred, James trained at Scarborough Technical College, before moving to London to work at some of the city's best restaurants, followed by a spell at Chewton Glen as junior pastry chef. He became Head Chef of Hotel du Vin in Winchester in 1994, and then the Talbot Hotel in 2012. In 2013 he opened James Martin Manchester, and in 2017 opened The Kitchen Cookery School and restaurant at Chewton Glen.

- *Cheese & Tomato Quiche (see page 48)*
- *Lamb Boulangère with Vegetables – Family-style (see page 154)*

THOMASINA MIERS

After learning to cook at her mother's side, Thomasina experimented with various careers before Clarissa Dickson Wright encouraged her to attend cookery school. Having travelled to Mexico to open a cocktail bar, she was inspired by the diversity and quality of the country's ingredients. When she came to open her own restaurant back in the UK (following a spectacular *MasterChef* win), it was a natural fit and Wahaca was born.

- *Meat-free Chilli with Roast Roots & Beans (see page 70)*
- *Steak & Cheese Tacos (see page 164)*

SAIPHIN MOORE

Saiphin was taught to cook by her mother and aunts in her native Thailand, and aged just 14 set up a noodle shop. After moving to Hong Kong and working as a nanny, Saiphin opened a Thai grocery shop and takeaway. In 2006 she moved to London with her husband, Alex, and ran a catering business during the week while running a Thai food stall in Brick Lane at the weekends. In 2008 she opened Rosa's Thai, which now has 18 sites across the UK.

- *Spicy Beef Salad (see page 66)*
- *Chilli, Basil & Minced Pork Stir Fry (see page 182)*

NAVED NASIR

After training in New Delhi and becoming one of India's youngest Executive Chefs, Naved moved from Bombay to the UK in 2010 to open the first Dishoom café with Shamil and Kavi Thakrar. The team now have eight restaurants in the UK, all of which pay loving homage to the Irani cafés of Bombay.

- *Chilli Broccoli Salad (see page 60)*
- *Dishoom's Chilli Chicken (see page 144)*

CHANTELLE NICHOLSON

Born in New Zealand, Chantelle trained as a lawyer before discovering her passion for food. Through the Gordon Ramsay Scholarship competition, she met Josh Emett, Head Chef of The Savoy Grill by Marcus Wareing, who offered her a job. She moved to London and quickly rose through the ranks. In 2014 she opened Tredwells with Marcus, taking sole ownership in 2017.

- *Roasted Aubergine with Harissa & Sesame (see page 72)*
- *Autumn Vegetable Savoury Bread Pudding (see page 106)*

JAMIE OLIVER

Essex-born Jamie grew up in the family pub, The Cricketers, where he was soon to be found in the kitchen. He joined Antonio Carluccio's Neal Street restaurant as a pastry chef, where he met his mentor Gennaro Contaldo, before taking on the role of Sous Chef at the River Café. Alongside his campaigning, Jamie has set up many restaurants across the world.

- *Corner-shop Curry Sauce – use it your way (see page 142)*
- *Eggless Chocolate Cake (see page 206)*

ADAM O'SHEPHERD

Adam worked in the restaurant industry for 20 years before stepping out of the kitchen and turning his hand to restaurant consultancy, food styling and recipe development. He recipe tested and styled all the recipes in this book. His first book, *MasterChef Green*, is to be published in April 2021.

NATHAN OUTLAW

Despite having grown up in landlocked Maidstone, Kent, Nathan is hailed as the king of fish. Inspired by his father, Nathan was soon working in kitchens. After two years at college, he moved to London and then set his sights on Cornwall where he worked under Rick Stein. He went on to open Restaurant Nathan Outlaw, which, in 2020, became Outlaw's New Road. He also runs Outlaw's Fish Kitchen in Port Isaac.

- *Fish & Chips with Mushy Peas (see page 122)*
- *Baked Rice Pudding with Tropical Fruit Salsa (see page 198)*

GORDON RAMSAY

Injury meant that Gordon put aside his aspirations to become a footballer, and instead went back to college and completed a course in hotel management, which led him to train with some of the world's greatest chefs, including Albert Roux, Marco Pierre White and Joël Robuchon. In 1998 he opened Restaurant Gordon Ramsay and now has 35 restaurants internationally.

- *Chicken Schnitzel (see page 136)*
- *Banana Bread (see page 236)*

SIMON RIMMER

Having originally studied fashion and textile design, Simon later taught himself to cook. In 1990 he bought Greens, a vegetarian restaurant, despite having no professional culinary experience. Greens is now a thriving restaurant, where Simon works in the kitchen, training new staff and creating new dishes. He also has other sites across Manchester and Liverpool.

- *Gnocchi with Mushroom Ragù (see page 110)*
- *Vegan Toffee & Banana Pudding (see page 196)*

MICHEL ROUX JR

Born into a culinary dynasty, and having grown up in the kitchen his father worked in, Michel was always destined to be a chef. Michel trained at some of France's best restaurants, and after a stint at the Mandarin Hotel in Hong Kong, he returned to London to work at La Tante Claire before joining the family business. In 1991 he took over the running of Le Gavroche, continuing the work of his late father, Albert Roux, and late uncle, Michel, offering classic French cooking with a modern twist.

- *Lyonnaise Onion Soup (see page 58)*
- *Hot Pears with Blue Cheese & Walnuts (see page 220)*

VIVEK SINGH

While growing up in India and with food central to everyday life, Vivek soon fell in love with the sights, sounds and celebration of food, happily embracing the mix of cultures and cuisines. He is now the Executive Chef and CEO of four restaurants in London, including The Cinnamon Club, and one in Oxford, where he marries Indian spices and flavours with Western techniques and ingredients.

- *Masala Roti with Turmeric & Chilli Scrambled Eggs (see page 50)*
- *Lentil & Basmati Kichri with Burnt Aubergine Relish (see page 96)*

CLARE SMYTH

Growing up on a farm in Northern Ireland, it was a holiday job in a local restaurant that inspired Clare's love of cooking. She moved to England aged 16 to study catering, before training at some of the most celebrated kitchens in the world. She became Chef Patron at Restaurant Gordon Ramsay, and in 2017 Clare opened Core, with an emphasis on natural, sustainable British produce.

- *Charred Chilli Chicken with Jasmine Rice (see page 134)*
- *Warm Chocolate & Lavender Tart (see page 210)*

JACK STEIN

Born in Cornwall, a passion for food is in Jack's blood, and he enjoyed travelling the world with his parents and brothers as a boy. He started working as a kitchen porter and then waiter, before he entered the family business as Commis Chef after graduating from university. He has since worked at restaurants across the world, including Tetsuya's in Sydney. In 2017 Jack became Chef Director of the Rick Stein Restaurant Group.

- *Langoustine Linguine with Gochujang (see page 86)*
- *Sea Bass with Braised Shallots, Spinach & Beurre Blanc (see page 118)*

FAROKH TALATI

Having worked as a chef since he was 16, Farokh has travelled across the world, working with Angela Hartnett, Heston Blumenthal and the legendary Fergus Henderson. Now Head Chef of St John Bread and Wine, Farokh also hosts a monthly Parsi feast at Maison Bertaux, celebrating his Parsi heritage and cultural traditions.

- *Parsi Omelette (see page 14)*
- *Butternut Squash & Coconut Curry (see page 100)*

STEPHEN TERRY

Chef Patron of The Hardwick in Abergavenny, Stephen has worked with some of the best chefs in the world. Mentored by Marco Pierre White and then working under Michel Roux Jr at Le Gavroche and in Paris with Alain Passard, Stephen returned to the UK and moved to south Wales, opening The Hardwick with his wife, Joanna.

- *A Kind of Spanish Toad in the Hole (see page 180)*
- *Chocolate Mousse with my Favourite Candy Bars (see page 192)*

BEN TISH

Classically trained, with over 20 years' experience, Ben spent his formative career working at various ground-breaking restaurants, before heading up his own operations at Al Duca and the Crinan Hotel. He is now the Culinary Director of The Stafford Collection, overseeing their offerings at the Stafford Hotel and its restaurant, Norma.

- *Rigatoni with Cavolo Nero, Pecorino & Pangrattato (see page 114)*
- *Warm Black Fig and Almond Puddings with Whipped Mascarpone (see page 214)*

CYRUS TODIWALA

Born in Bombay, Cyrus became the Executive Chef of the Taj Group in Goa before leaving India for Australia. He moved to London where he opened Namasté restaurant, blending traditional Indian techniques with unexpected ingredients. He is Proprietor and Executive Chef of Café Spice Namasté, Mr Todiwala's Kitchen at both the Hilton T5 and The Curio by Hilton Canary Wharf, and Mr Todiwala's Petiscos in Essex.

- *1833 Cheese Bites (see page 34)*
- *Spiced Mixed Berry, Walnut, Rum & Port Cake (see page 240)*

MITCH TONKS

It was in his grandmother's Weston-super-Mare kitchen that Mitch fell in love with food, especially fish and shellfish. At The Seahorse, the Dartmouth restaurant he co-owns with Mat Prowse, and at Rockfish, his seafood restaurant chain, Mitch's ethos of keeping it simple is key, embracing freshness and flavour.

- *White Beans & Mussels with Wild Fennel Aioli (see page 80)*
- *Espresso Panna Cotta (see page 228)*

GARY USHER & RICHARD SHARPLES

Born in St Albans and raised in north Wales, Gary spent time in the kitchens of Chapter One, Chez Bruce and The Chester Grosvenor before opening Sticky Walnut in 2011. Taking the unique step of crowd-funding further restaurants, Gary has since opened five bistros across the north west of England with Richard Sharples as his right-hand man, all of which are in the *Good Food Guide*.

- *Spiced Roast Chicken with Chips & Peas (see page 138)*
- *Custard Tart (see page 208)*

MARCUS WAREING

The son of a fruit and veg merchant, Marcus began his career aged 18, working in many of London's top restaurants with Anton Edelmann, Albert Roux and Gordon Ramsay before founding Marcus Wareing Restaurants in 2008 with wife Jane.

- *Chilled Garden Soup with Smoked Salmon & Crème Fraîche (see page 56)*
- *Sausage & Lentil Casserole (see page 176)*

JOHN WILLIAMS

Having grown up in South Shields as a fisherman's son and cooking alongside his mother, John moved to London to work at the Royal Garden Hotel, the Berkeley and Claridge's before taking the helm as Executive Chef at The Ritz hotel, offering the finest ingredients cooked in the finest style.

- *My Home Niçoise Salad (see page 64)*
- *Bakewell Tart (see page 230)*

ANDREW WONG

Andrew's parents owned a restaurant where he spent much of his childhood. On the death of his father, Andrew returned to help his mother run the restaurant, and developed a love for the traditional and regional cuisines of China, travelling the country to learn the various techniques. On his return to London, Andrew reopened the restaurant as A Wong (named for his parents, Albert and Annie), fusing Chinese cooking techniques with his classical training.

- *Yangzhou Fried Rice (see page 82)*
- *Singapore Noodles (see page 178)*

About Hospitality Action

Hospitality Action was established in 1837 and has since offered vital assistance to all who work, or have worked within hospitality in the UK.

We're here for the chefs, waiters, housekeepers and managers. We're here for the concierges, receptionists and kitchen porters. And we're here for every sommelier, bartender, catering assistant and cook across the UK.

Whether it's for people who work in hotels, restaurants, pubs, bars or cafés, schools, hospitals or event venues, we're here to give them the help, advice and support they need whenever times get tough.

From physical illness or mental health issues to financial difficulty, family problems or addiction, Hospitality Action is here to get hospitality staff back on their feet again. And when it's no longer possible to work, we can help them prepare for the next phase of their life.

There are so many ways to support our work, and many reasons to do so. Contact us, or find out more on our website.

To all of you in the industry, we've got you.

hospitalityaction.org.uk
Registered Charity No. 1101083

Acknowledgements

We would like to thank all the chefs involved in the making of this book, contributing their time and mouth-watering recipes in aid of a very good cause. This book would be impossible without your incredible support and generosity, and we are proud to be the charity that serves your industry.

A thank you must also go to Kris Kirkham for the glorious photography within these pages and Adam O'Shepherd for a heroic effort styling the recipes on shoot, which was done in a short amount of time and without assistance due to Covid-19 restrictions.

And thank you to David Loftus for stepping in when Covid lockdowns meant that we couldn't photograph all the recipes, producing the beautiful illustrations in the book.

Publisher
Jon Croft

Commissioning Editor
Meg Boas

Project Editor
Emily North

Hospitality Action Project Management
Mark Lewis & Astrid Wears-Taylor

Art Direction & Cover Design
Marie O'Shepherd

Art Direction & Design
Peter Moffat

Junior Designer
Anika Schulze

Food Styling & Home Economy
Adam O'Shepherd

Photography
Kris Kirkham

Photographer's Assistant
Eyder Rosso

Illustration
David Loftus

Copyeditor
Judy Barratt

Proofreader
Rachel Malig

Indexer
Zoe Ross

Cover props kindly donated by
China & Co (Props Hire) Limited

Linen props supplied by
Wilbur & Wolf – The Linen & Prop Store

First published in Great Britain by
Jon Croft Editions in 2021
info@joncrofteditions.com
www.joncrofteditions.com

ISBN: 9780993354038

Reprinted three times in March 2021.

Printed and bound in the UK for Gomer Press Wales.

MIX
Paper from
responsible sources
FSC® C114687
FSC
www.fsc.org

Contributor's portraits, back cover and pages 8-9:
Paul Ainsworth © Andrew Callaghan, Jason Atherton © Nikki To, Sat Bains © John
Arandhara-Blackwell, Tommy Banks © Andrew Hayes-Watkins, Nieves Barragán
Mohacho, Ellis Barrie, Raymond Blanc © Paul Wilkinson, Heston Blumenthal © John
Scott Blackwell, Claude Bosi, Tom Brown © Ed Schofield, Michael Caines, Claire
Clark © André Bieganski, Daniel Clifford, James Cochran, Richard Corrigan, Jon Croft
© Emily North, Thuy Diem Pham © Nick Gommon, Calum Franklin © John Carey,
Chris Galvin, Robin Gill © Paul Winch-Furness, Lisa Goodwin-Allen © Allen Markey,
Elizabeth Haigh © Pomme Hongsananda, Angela Hartnett, Anna Haugh, Mark Hix,
Phil Howard © Andrew Hayes-Watkins, Niall Keating © Adrian Franklin, Tom Kerridge
© Cristian Barnett, Selin Kiazim, Kris Kirkham © Kris Kirkham, Tom Kitchin © Marc
Millar, Atul Kochhar, Mark Lewis, Giorgio Locatelli, David Loftus © David Loftus, Nokx
Majozi © John Carey, James Martin, Thomasina Miers © Tara Fisher, Saiphin Moore ©
Alex Maguire, Naved Nasir © Jon Cottam, Chantelle Nicholson, Jamie Oliver © Jamie
Oliver Enterprises Ltd, photography by David Loftus, Adam O'Shepherd © Adam
O'Shepherd, Nathan Outlaw © David Loftus, Gordon Ramsay, Simon Rimmer, Michel
Roux Jr © Jodi Hinds, Vivek Singh © Lara Holmes, Clare Smyth © Core by Clare Smyth,
Jack Stein © David Griffen, Farokh Talati © Sam A Harris, Stephen Terry © Michelle
Martin, Ben Tish © Kris Kirkham, Cyrus Todiwala, Mitch Tonks, Gary Usher and Richard
Sharples © Allen Markey, Marcus Wareing, John Williams, Andrew Wong © Jutta Klee